A Spirituality for Contemporary Life

A Spirituality for Contemporary Life
The Jesuit Heritage Today

Edited by David L. Fleming, S.J.

Review for Religious
St. Louis

© 1991 Review for Religious
All rights reserved
Printed in the United States of America

Review for Religious
3601 Lindell Boulevard
St. Louis, Missouri 63108

ISBN 0-924768-02-9

The cover design is modeled on the Ignatian lecture series brochure designed by Laura Calvo de Luis. Special thanks to Mary Flick and the Saint Louis University Department of Publications.

Ad majorem Dei gloriam

Acknowledgments

Review for Religious is privileged to publish this book on contemporary Ignatian spirituality. The origin of the book was the Ignatian lecture series, presented in February and March 1991 and jointly sponsored by the Saint Louis University's Ignatian Anniversaries committee, the College of Arts and Sciences, the Department of Theological Studies, the Jesuit Community at Saint Louis University, St. Francis Xavier (College) Church, Aquinas Institute of Theology, the Institute of Jesuit Sources, *Review for Religious*, and *Theology Digest*. J. J. Mueller, S.J., and Mary Lea Reuter, O.S.B., coordinated the planning and execution of the lecture series.

The preparation of the manuscripts for book form has been done by the staff of *Review for Religious*. I want to express my gratitude to Philip Fischer, S.J., Mrs. Mary Ann Foppe, Michael Harter, S.J., and Miss Jean Read, who added the preparation of these manuscripts to their everyday responsibilities. I also add a special thanks to Tracy Gramm, Michael Harter, S.J., and Thomas Rochford, S.J., for the design and format of this publication.

I hope that this book, by its careful development in written form of the original oral text, will enrich all those who by their presence enthusiastically supported the lecture series, the faculty and friends of Saint Louis University, the readers of *Review for Religious*, and all others who seek a deeper understanding and appreciation of the spiritual legacy of St. Ignatius Loyola and the Jesuit Order which he founded.

David L. Fleming, S.J.
Editor

Contents

viii
Foreword
J. J. Mueller, S.J.

1
The Richness of a Resource
Walter J. Burghardt, S.J.

21
Finding a Busy God
David L. Fleming, S.J.

31
Christian Responsibility for Today's World
Monika K. Hellwig

44
Rich and Poor Churches and the Compassion Principle
Jon Sobrino, S.J.

64
The Greater Glory of God: Woman Fully Alive
Elizabeth A. Johnson, C.S.J.

82
God's Search Goes On
John W. Padberg, S.J.

Foreword

THE IGNATIAN YEAR celebrates the 450th anniversary of the founding of the Society of Jesus and the 500th anniversary of the birth of Ignatius Loyola. To mark this occasion, a lecture series emerged as a bright idea at the end of a long afternoon meeting in the Theological Studies Department at Saint Louis University. Like many ideas hastily concocted at the end of a meeting, no one knew if it would ever come to light. Such ideas need moral and mental support, and money as well. But thanks to the joint sponsorship of the Dominicans of Aquinas Institute of Theology, Saint Louis University's Ignatian Anniversaries committee, the College of Arts and Sciences, the Jesuit Community at Saint Louis University, St. Francis Xavier (College) Church, the Institute of Jesuit Sources, *Review for Religious*, and *Theology Digest*, the idea found its life supports. An "ecumenical" gathering of academics, publishers, parishioners, religious, and laity formed a community of committed concern, and in the months ahead this group provided a resource and richness that was continually drawn upon.

The recently deceased and much-beloved general of the Society of Jesus, Pedro Arrupe, was fond of saying in his Basque English, "Yes, but how to do?" How could we make the lecture-series idea work? How could we manage to speak about Ignatius and his "company," their history and their identity, in a fresh way? One does not examine any heritage simply to return to the past, but to look to the past to retrieve what is richest and then move into the future. The Jesuit heritage is something that must serve others. Thus the theme of the series took clearer focus: how could the Jesuit heritage help Jesuits and others to reinvigorate their spiritual and apostolic life? True to the Jesuit charism and to the inspiration of Father Arrupe's dynamic practicality, the title of the series became "A Spirituality for Contemporary Life: The Jesuit Heritage Today."

In a real sense the planning committee became an image of what we were trying to help others do: work together for the good of others. Our individual and group creativity was challenged to come up with lecturers and topics that could fulfill and even extend our dream. From the start we encouraged the speakers to approach the Ignatian heritage creatively, to push the "edge of the envelope," to venture into new and uncharted waters. Our six lecturers, we think, did so.

They gave their lectures in the St. Francis Xavier (College) Church at Saint Louis University. One year ago the College Church began a beautiful renovation, completed only months before the series began. Although we had planned to have the lectures in a large university assembly hall, a representative of the College Church approached us and suggested our using the church. The suggestion fitted the series wonderfully. The renovated lighting system enhanced the neo-Gothic lines of the 1884 church, creating an aesthetically soothing and yet transcendent space at the same time. A Lenten lecture series in the church, Ignatian Anniversaries celebrated in a religious setting—the lecture series would not have been the same if we had not been in a place of prayer. The lectures breathe prayer, while being academically and aesthetically pleasing presentations. You will pick this up as you read.

After each lecture we reserved a period of time for audience responses. This time was not a question-and-answer period but a sharing of experience. Perhaps we were all awkward at first, but we learned quickly and willingly. The audience's responses, or testimonials, were insightful ("the Eucharist is a feminine symbol because Jesus feeds us from his own body"), contributive ("this is the first time as a male I've felt included in a discussion on women"), at times pain-filled ("I feel the oppression of the Church and don't want to support a dysfunctional family, yet want to stay"), searching ("comfort seems to make us inaccessible to God"), but remarkably accepting ("as a black American, I want to forgive my oppressors"). Each evening throughout the six weeks, we formed a community of listening, acceptance, challenge, and openness to God. And judging from the stories related to me, I believe that true conversion experiences occurred. Something extraordinary happened here, and the catalysts were the outstanding lecturers.

Walter Burghardt began the series with "The Richness of a Resource." As teacher, scholar, editor, he has contributed to the landscape of American theology for over half a century. His scholarly interests began in studying early Church history, continued in his teaching at Woodstock College, and found expression in his editing of *Theological Studies* for forty-six years. Known also for his work in homiletics, he has contributed significantly to the relationship of preaching and spirituality through his many books, such as *Seasons that Laugh or Weep*. Now as director of the program "Preaching the Just Word" at Manresa-on-Severn, he draws from his many years of experience in a creative effort to move social issues more effectively into Catholic pulpits of the country. In addressing the topic of "The Richness of a Resource" he focuses upon religious experience as the beginning point and confirming affirmation of spirituality today.

Editor of *Review for Religious*, David Fleming is known for his conferences, workshops, and writing in the areas of Jesuit spirituality, spiritual direction, and religious life. A former professor of theology at Saint Louis University and Weston School of Theology in Boston, former provincial of the Missouri Province, and current superior of the Jesuit collegiate formation program, he has authored several books on the *Spiritual Exercises* of St. Ignatius and coedited a book entitled *Religious Life: Rebirth Through Conversion*. His "How to Find a Busy God" focuses on how God works for us.

Professor of religious studies at Georgetown, former president of the Catholic Theological Society of America, Monika Hellwig has also won the prestigious John Courtney Murray award for her outstanding contribution to American theology. Her long-standing relationship with the Jesuit heritage and her creative advancement as a laywoman contribute to her treatment of "Christian Responsibility for Today's World." In constant demand as a lecturer, she has authored fifteen books and more than a hundred articles. With a strong pastoral concern and clear writing style, she has become a leading interpreter of the Catholic tradition for contemporary Christianity.

An alumnus of Saint Louis University, Jon Sobrino delivered the fourth lecture and packed the church to bulging. His book *Christology at the Crossroads* has made a major impact on theology worldwide. His theology and life are characterized by a strong social involvement with and for the poor of El Salvador. A professor of theology at the University of Central America in San Salvador, he directs the Monsignor Romero Center and coedits a journal of Latin American theology. His twelve books and numerous articles have been translated into several languages. Had he not been out of the country November 16, 1989, he would have been with his six Jesuit colleagues and the two laywomen who were slain on the university grounds. His topic, "Rich and Poor Churches and the Compassion Principle," challenges the U.S. perception of the world and its standards.

A professor of theology at Catholic University of America, Elizabeth Johnson is known as an outstanding teacher and scholar. She has written a number of articles on feminist theology, the nature of religious language, as well as on the doctrine of God, Jesus, Mary, and the saints. She serves on a variety of committees and is a consultant to the national Lutheran/Roman Catholic dialogue, the National Conference of Catholic Bishops, and an international committee on the use of English in the liturgy. Her work consistently combines a deep understanding of the Christian tradition and its riches for life today. Her "The Greater Glory of God: Woman Fully Alive" extends the Ignatian heritage in ways that would both please and astound St. Ignatius.

Scholar, teacher, administrator, and editor characterize the final lecturer, John Padberg. Currently director of the Institute of Jesuit Sources, which publishes scholarly work on Jesuit tradition worldwide, he also chairs the Seminar on Jesuit Spirituality and a newly formed Seminar on Jesuit Higher Education. He edits the journal *Studies in the Spirituality of Jesuits*. His scholarship on the history of the Jesuits is internationally recognized, and he is in constant demand as a leading articulator of Jesuit tradition. His lecture, "God's Search Goes On," examines the changes in the contemporary world and the challenges they bring to retrieving a spirituality applicable for tomorrow.

Before the series began, one administrator cautioned, "People don't attend lectures anymore." The attendance was astounding, averaging about five hundred people each evening; some three thousand attended these lectures. The audience included people from Africa, the Philippines, South America, and the Orient. Without doubt, something special happened. The lecturers catalyzed the community to examine their own experiences, deal with the challenges of the Jesuit heritage, and look to God beckoning them into the future. Not expectedly, each lecturer remarked about the attentive and interactive nature of the community present. The interrelation of the lecturers and the audience bears fruit in the written texts, especially because most of the talks were revised in light of the presentation. The audience clearly drew out the best from the lecturers, who recognized a receptive audience.

This time of celebrating anniversaries is a time for memories, a time to retrieve what is best in our spirituality in order to contribute to a new, creative life. We do not hold the future—that is God's creative and mysterious design; but we do hold the past. We build on the human side, but rely on the divine. In these lectures you will find the divine calling to us, for the Holy Spirit continues to "renew the face of the earth" while never forsaking the richness of the past.

J. J. Mueller, S.J.

J.J. Mueller, S.J., is associate professor in the Department of Theological Studies at Saint Louis University. He was chair of the committee and coordinator of the Ignatian Anniversaries Lecture Series.

The Richness of a Resource
Walter J. Burghardt, S.J.

FIVE HUNDRED YEARS have fled since Iñigo de Loyola was born into this world, 451 years since his society was solemnly confirmed by Pope Paul III, 435 years since he breathed his last. Since then, the world has changed drastically. Ecumenical man and woman are not Reformation and Counter-Reformation male and female. The earth is no longer flat, the universe geocentric. Palestrina has yielded pride of place to Red Hot Chili Peppers. America has been discovered, and the Gateway to the West is not Spain but St. Louis. The Scholasticism that fed Ignatius and his first followers has been swallowed up by existentialism, process philosophy and theology, logical analysis. The medieval marriage of the world with Christ has given way to an "eclipse of God," "an absence [of God] from consciousness . . . within great masses of people."[1]

Given such profound change, what can "the Jesuit heritage" in spirituality possibly have to say to contemporary man and woman which is not proposed more attractively by Thomas Merton and Mother Teresa, by Anne Carr and Joann Conn, by John Powell and Teilhard de Chardin? Why go back to a dead past when the living present is so rich, so inviting? Lovers of our national pastime do not emulate Ty Cobb when Rickie Henderson is around stealing bases. Theater folk admire Laurence Olivier musing in the forties on the burdens of kings, but plunk down their dollars to watch Kenneth Branagh play Henry V for our time. Sophocles and Cicero are nice to read if you have the leisure, but it's an M.B.A. that puts the turkey on the table for economic man and economic woman. Heritages are "hot stuff" for historians, but really, who can afford to live off them?

I do not propose to deplore what we have dismissed, lust for a lost Eden, implore you to live in 1491, canonize a static traditionalism. I shall stress a living tradition. And a living tradition I define as the best of the past, infused with the insights of the present, with a view to a more fruitful future. In this light I shall argue that a recent emphasis in theology and philosophy has roots in Ignatian spirituality and those roots deserve to be brought into your present. I am speaking of experience. For sweet clarity's sake, let me develop my thesis through three questions: (1) What is experience? (2) How does experience relate to Ignatian spirituality? (3) Where might you and I insert all this into contemporary Christian living, into your spirituality and mine?

First, experience itself. As I was growing up, and deep into the sixties, the word "experience" was a Catholic no-no. Experience had a bastard ancestry: it was presumably born of Protestant parents in the sixteenth century and reborn in the petri dish of twentieth-century Modernism. The background merits more than brief mention; otherwise we risk the danger of oversimplifying.

Aside from Catholicism, one common note characterizes the four centuries of Western Christianity from Luther to William James: the ultimate criterion and rule of faith is religious experience. To it all else must yield: dogma, authority, speculative reason.[2] Several examples may clarify a complex phenomenon.

1. For Luther, with his conviction that Adam's sin meant total corruption of human nature, religion is my first experience of my own sinfulness, of a justification that comes to me from outside myself, because God attributes to me the merits of Christ. Though purely passive, I still experience a personal conviction that I am saved. What is faith? Not belief in dogmas but a kind of confidence, of trust.

2. For Danish philosopher and theologian Søren Kierkegaard, in anguish and despair I become aware of my own insufficiency, and in this way I am

> led to religious experience that consists in an act of commitment to

God. This act rests upon an awareness of God that amounts to a personal encounter; historical faith is of no avail here, and the experience cannot be rendered in concepts. Ultimate truth is pure subjectivity, demanding that God "break in" upon the soul.[3]

3. The movement called Modernism is too complex to summarize here.[4] Suffice it to say that, for some of the Modernists, the only way ultimately to measure the validity of faith is human experience; belief must be measured by human response.

I submit that, justified as we Catholics are in rejecting "pure subjectivity" in religion, a misplaced stress on *sola experientia* (experience and nothing but experience), we have once again thrown out the baby with the bath water. Indeed we cannot jettison dogmas declared by a divinely directed Church. Indeed Catholic faith is more than sheer trust, it includes a loving acceptance of what God has revealed in Christ. Indeed there is such a thing as objective truth, truth that does not depend for its existence on whether I am thinking about it. And still it is a mistake, as John Courtney Murray saw, to conceive objective truth as existing "already out there now," apart from its possession by anyone, apart from history, "formulated in propositions that are verbally immutable." In contrast to such a "classical" view of truth,

> historical consciousness, while holding fast to the nature of truth as objective, is concerned with the possession of truth, with man's affirmations of truth, with the understanding contained in these affirmations, with the conditions—both circumstantial and subjective—of understanding and affirmation, and therefore with the historicity of truth and with progress in the grasp and penetration of what is true.[5]

Put more simply, objective truth does not exist in midair; it has to be experienced; a subject has to grasp it. If truth is unchanging, "in the concrete, [our] struggle to understand is not static and unchanging"; in the flesh-and-blood world our "point of view, experience, conceptions, and language change," and so our "grasp of 'truths' . . . changes, too."[6]

Given this background, it is high time to reopen the basic question: Precisely what is this creature called experience?[7] Begin with sheerly human experience. Not everything I sense qualifies as a genuine experience. Simply to see the sun rise, to hear Tchaikovsky's *Swan Lake*, to shake another's hand, to smell new-mown grass, to taste oysters Rockefeller—this is not yet authentic experience. I must encounter the real in a way that leads me to respond to it and to appropriate that encounter critically as an event in my personal history.

Examples? Take poet Robert Lowell cruelly kidded by classmates ("Dimbulb," "Droopy-drawers") and carrying the scars for life:

> I was fifteen;
> They made me cry in public.[8]

Take French writer Simone Weil. In her early teens she was keenly troubled by a sense of unworthiness (her brother was a mathematical prodigy); she was never to forget a remark she overheard from a visitor to her mother: the boy "is genius itself," the girl is "beauty." And forever after this singularly gifted woman did her best to destroy what was superficially charming in her, putting to death sheer beauty with shapeless clothes, clumsy gestures, unmusical voice.[9] Take John Merrick, "the elephant man," grossly misshapen, shunned like a leper, housed like a wild beast, but transformed when a young widow entered his room, wished him good morning, and shook his hand. He sobbed uncontrollably; apart from his mother, this was the first woman who had ever smiled at him, had ever touched his hand. From then on he lost his shyness, loved to see his door open and the world flock to him: "I am happy every hour of the day."[10]

A special dimension of human experience is the religious. It opens you up "to a new world of meaning and a new way of understanding [your]self and reality in relation to the sacred."[11] What is this "new world of meaning"? It is a world whose center is God: God transcendent and God immanent. Transcendent: I mean God as he exists in his essential nature, prior to the world, exalted above the world, having real existence whether the world thinks of him or not. Immanent: I mean God indwelling in the world, especially in man and woman. What is the "new way of understanding [your]self and reality in relation" to God? It is

> some sort of awareness of and response to the divine, largely achieved in terms of discerning the divine presence or one's total dependence upon divinity. This may be immediate or mediated, but is necessarily subjective either entirely so or with varying degrees of foundation in external reality and history. It is in opposition to abstract rational thought and not infrequently accompanied by such phenomena as revelation, inspiration, voices and visions, conversion, etc.[12]

How do we actually experience reality?[13] Most obviously, through the five senses: I see a sunrise, I hear Beethoven's *Mass in D*, I touch a face I love, I taste veal piccata, I smell a rose. Now sense experience is not what we mean when we speak of an experience of *God*. Sense experiences are incredibly important: they can lead us to a reflective awareness of God, and through sense experiences like the sacraments God's presence is mediated to our lives. So, hold on to sense experience; hold on to it literally "for your life." But, properly speaking, this is not what theologians and spiritual writers ordinarily mean by the expression "experience of God."

A second way we experience reality, encounter the real, is by grasping it intellectually, with our minds. I grapple with ideas in a book of theology, read the *Post-Dispatch* to learn the latest about war or civil unrest, engage in conversation about the stock market, about ethics, even about God. By using my God-given intelligence, I can indeed fashion ideas, concepts, about God: God is good, all-powerful, forgiving; God is Love. But here I do not grasp God directly. Oh, I say correctly, "God is good," but immediately I must add, "but not as humans are good"—in a way, actually, that totally transcends human goodness. Our concepts, our ideas, do not grasp God as God is in Godself.

> *The love that 'believes all things, hopes all things, endures all things, never ends.'*

But if neither senses nor intellect can experience God directly, does that leave us with no possibility of experiencing God? Fortunately, no. There are deeper experiences that occur on a level beyond senses and beyond concepts.

Take two examples from our own very human existence: beauty and love. I listen to Beethoven's *Symphony No. 9*, specifically his "Ode to Joy." To hear the individual notes, I depend on my senses, on my hearing. To "grasp the conceptual order of the music and the interrelationship of part and whole," I use my intellect. And yet I experience "a beauty which transcends the faculties of hearing and thought. The beauty of the symphony is beyond logic," and I know that what I experience "cannot adequately be reduced to concepts or words."[14] That which is most profound in what I experience I cannot verbalize.

If I love you, my love has to be shaped of sense experience: how I see you, hear you, touch you. And it stems in large measure from understanding: how my intelligence grasps what is more profound in you than your qualifications for Miss America. But the love that St. Paul sings, the love that "believes all things, hopes all things, endures all things, never ends" (1 Cor 13:7, 8), the love that Christ exemplified, love unto crucifixion—such love I despair of expressing.

It is the mystery dimension of human knowing and loving. It pervades your life: the inexpressible experience that is the birth of your child; artistic creation in song and sculpture, in drama and dance; your rapture in a star-packed sky and the sweet single note of a wood thrush. Such experience, beyond the reach of the empirical and the rational, is the experience of God. In this life our senses and our intellect cannot penetrate to God's inner being. God remains mystery; but it is precisely as mystery that we can experience God's presence and action.

Such opening up, such awareness, such response is not something you can manufacture by your human powers of knowing and loving, not something you can acquire by willing it. It is a gift. For in genuinely religious experience you are aware not only of the mysterious, such as another's psyche, the flight of two hundred billion billion stars, the chemistry of love. You are aware of Mystery, capital M. Mystery that is Life, capital L. Mystery that is Love, capital L. Mystery that is Trinity. Mystery that is God in flesh. Mystery that is God within you. To remove this from outer space, to concretize it, I move on to my second main point.

How DOES EXPERIENCE RELATE TO IGNATIAN SPIRITUALITY? I begin with a fascinating facet of Ignatius's Spiritual Exercises that is frequently forgotten or simply overlooked. An Ignatian retreat (at its best, thirty days of meditation, contemplation) is not a head trip, much as the intellect is involved. It is an experience, a lived and living experience. I not only come face-to-face with the objective face of the real, with truth somewhere out there. Reality, truth, is something I grasp by living in it, living it.[15] Ignatius would resonate to Whitehead: "the living organ of experience is the living body as a whole."[16]

This includes in a significant way the five sense organs as avenues of communication with the external world. Take Ignatius's meditation on the Incarnation, the glad tidings brought to Mary. You are asked to *look*: join the Trinity in looking "down upon the whole expanse or circuit of all the earth." You are asked to see

> those on the face of the earth, in such great diversity in dress and

in manner of acting. Some are white, some black; some at peace, and some at war; some weeping, some laughing; some well, some sick; some coming into the world, and some dying; etc.[17]

You are asked to *listen*: listen to men and women swearing and blaspheming; listen to Father, Son, and Spirit saying, "Let us work the redemption of the human race"; listen to Gabriel telling Mary, "You will conceive," listen to Mary responding, "Let it happen to me as you say."[18] In the meditation on hell you are asked to *smell*: smell "the smoke, the sulphur, the filth, and corruption."[19] You are asked to *taste*: "taste the bitterness of tears, sadness, and remorse of conscience."[20] You are asked to *touch*: "feel the flames."[21] In Ignatius's Spiritual Exercises, what he calls "the application of the senses" is of high importance. To keep meditation from turning into abstract thought, you must feel. You sweat as Christ sweats blood in the garden; you cringe under the lashes that tear his back; your lips grow dry when he murmurs, "I thirst" (Jn 19:28). And to help you rejoice in the risen Christ, Ignatius suggests, "make use of the light and the pleasures of the seasons—for example, in summer of the refreshing coolness, in the winter of the sun and fire."[22]

> *The psychology of Ignatian prayer puts the history of salvation into the present tense.*

Seeing and hearing, smelling and tasting and touching; this Ignatian application of the senses has two stages, two levels—not contradictory, not mutually exclusive, even if two distinct schools of thought have arisen in their regard.[23] First, there is a simpler stage, an almost primitive form of prayer of which almost anyone is capable. During a retreat Ignatius always had this take place

> in the evening, hence at a time when the exercitant could quietly and peacefully gather the threads of his earlier [four] meditations, a time when his soul had already been loosened up by the work of devoting the understanding and will to meditation and the search for the will of God. The evening was intended as a time of calm and composure, during which the soul could realize what Ignatius at the very beginning of the Exercises (2) had laid down as the essential aim to be achieved in all true prayer: "It is not extensive knowledge which fills and satisfies the soul, but rather the interior understanding of things and appreciation of them."[24]

Such appreciation through the senses introduces a significant facet of the psychology of prayer: putting the history of salvation into the present tense. What Christ said and did I see, I must see, as happening today; the events of his life I draw into my own world of the here and now.

But this application of my bodily senses should move me to a higher form of prayer, the spiritual senses of the human heart. When after strenuous hours of meditation I unlock my soul in the relaxed evening hour, I ought to abandon myself to God's contact, "feel" the things of God—the *sentir* fundamental to Ignatian prayer.[25] It is then that I hear the soundless syllables of God, taste God's sweetness. No one can teach me this; I have to experience it, and even then human language fails me. It is St. Augustine asking his God, "What do I love when I love you?" And he replies:

> When I love my God, I love a kind of light, a kind of voice, a kind of perfume, a kind of food, a kind of embrace—a light, a voice, a perfume, a food, an embrace of my inner self—where that shines in my soul which space cannot contain, where that sounds which time does not snatch away, where that fragrance breathes which no wind scatters, where that is tasted which no eating diminishes, an embrace which satiety does not sunder. This it is I love when I love my God.[26]

Here Augustine has moved beyond the five senses, beyond the power of sheer intellect to reach God. He has touched the pinnacle of prayer, the extreme of experience. Let's touch this "What do I love when I love my God?" to Ignatius. Given the importance of senses and intellect for religious experience, let me touch Augustine's "What do I love when I love my God?" to Ignatius's experience of God, the pinnacle of Ignatian experience. In a remarkable essay over a decade ago, "Ignatius of Loyola Speaks to a Modern Jesuit," Karl Rahner put on the lips of Ignatius a number of powerful affirmations based on his own profound insight into the saint. Among them, hear this:

> I was convinced that first, tentatively, during my illness in Loyola and then, decisively, during my time as a hermit in Manresa I had a direct encounter with God. This was the experience I longed to communicate to others, as far as I could.
>
> When I claim to have experienced God directly...I am not speaking of graphic visions, symbols, voices, not speaking of the gift of tears and suchlike. All I say is: I experienced God, nameless and unfathomable, silent and yet near, bestowing Himself upon me in His Trinity. I experienced God...beyond all concrete imaginings....
>
> I really encountered God, the true and living God....I experienced God Himself. Even then I could distinguish God in Himself from the words, the images, the limited individual experiences that

in some fashion point to God....God Himself. It was God's very self I experienced, not human words describing Him.... This experience is grace indeed, and basically there is no one to whom it is refused. Of this I was convinced.²⁷

What, concretely, did Ignatius experience? First, and centrally, an experience of the Blessed Trinity, which he saw as "three keys of an organ" or a musical chord, each note contributing to the perfect harmony of all three—this while praying on the steps of a Dominican monastery. "This mystery of the Trinity," John Padberg has said, "is sometimes so impoverished by speculation that it ends up almost a celestial algebra. For Ignatius, however, it became for his whole spiritual life that from which everything came and toward which everything returned in a perpetual movement and communication."²⁸

Ignatius's experiences were not classes in theology.

Second, as Ignatius put it in the third person, "there was represented to his understanding with great spiritual delight the manner in which God had created the world. It had the appearance of something white out of which rays were coming, and it was out of this that God made light."²⁹ Third, time and again Ignatius experienced the humanity of Jesus. At Manresa, he tells us, he saw the human Jesus "with interior eyes...many times...and each time for a long time."³⁰ Fourth, Ignatius experienced the Eucharist in so profound a way that the body of Christ would never again be a lifeless presence, always the radiant center of a world ceaselessly being created.³¹

Finally, in a sort of synthesis, on the banks of the River Cardoner, Ignatius had a single illumination—of God one and three, the world's fashioning, and the bodying forth of the Son—that outstripped, by his own admission, all he learned or was given by God in sixty-two years.³² It "may well be the most important event in Ignatius's life."³³

This does not mean that Ignatius suddenly became "some kind of walking encyclopedia."³⁴ These experiences were not classes in theology. They were not even, he asserted, "a vision, but [he came] to understand many things . . . with such clarity that everything appeared to him to be something new." And yet he found it impossible "to set down the details of all he understood then."³⁵ This we do know: The Cardoner experience altered his way of looking at all reality. The "holistic quality of this experience unified everything and put it in a new light."[36] But it did not leave him in outer space. It made for service of the poor, the sick, and the dying; it caused him to abandon excessive penances; it meant absolute trust in God's providence where food and clothing, shelter and finances were concerned.

Not only does Ignatius insist, "This remains certain: it is possible for the human person to experience God's very self."[37] He goes on to instruct us twentieth- and twenty-first-century Jesuits on the high importance of that conviction for the way we teach and preach to the lay faithful:

> Your pastoral care must keep this goal in mind always, at every step, inflexibly. If you fill up the barns of people's consciousness only with your ever-so-learned and up-to-date theology, in a way that ultimately generated no more than a frightful flood of words; if you were to train men and women merely for churchiness, as enthusiastic subjects of the ecclesiastical establishment; if in the Church you were to make people no more than obedient vassals of a distant God represented by an ecclesiastical magistracy; if you were not to help men and women through all these difficulties; if you were not to help them finally to let go of all tangible assurances and isolated insights and go with confidence toward that Inconceivable where there are no further ways, and to achieve this at the final, fearful, inescapable end of life and in the immeasurableness of love and joy and then radically and definitively in death (together with the Godforsaken dying Jesus), then you would have either forgotten or betrayed my "spirituality" in your so-called pastoral care and missionary apostolate.[38]

For Ignatius, nothing his sons can do for you takes precedence over this: to help you to an experience of God. This is not something Augustine or Ignatius could learn or put into understandable language. But it begins with the Ignatian effort to find God in all things. And that begins with sense experience, together with imagination, the capacity we all have "to make the material an image of the immaterial or spiritual."[39] It begins with an axiom from the medieval Scholastics: "There is nothing in our intellect that was not previously in our senses." Ignatius recognized that you and I are not disembodied intellects. Our ideas are triggered by sense experience—whether it's Alexander Fleming moving to penicillin from a mold growing on a culture of some common germs, or Ignatius rapt in ecstasy as he eyes the stars at night. It is the whole person, not only naked intellect, God has made in God's image; and it is the whole person, senses too, that must respond to the incredible world that surrounds us.

But we are not expected to stop with Ignatius. The Ignatian

heritage never stops growing, is ever open to further and further development. I submit that Ignatius would agree with a Whitehead paragraph on experience that has proved extraordinarily exciting and enriching to me:

> Nothing can be omitted, experience drunk and experience sober, experience sleeping and experience waking, experience drowsy and experience wideawake, experience self-conscious and experience self-forgetful, experience intellectual and experience physical, experience religious and experience skeptical, experience anxious and experience care-free, experience anticipatory and experience retrospective, experience happy and experience grieving, experience dominated by emotion and experience under self-restraint, experience in the light and experience in the dark, experience normal and experience abnormal.[40]

Over the years I have been broadened by what Whitehead calls "the main sources of evidence respecting this width of human experience." Three main sources: "language, social institutions, and action."[41] Oh yes, my experiential past did place strong stress on language, for example, concepts, definitions, deductions; but not stress enough on the "flashes of insight beyond meanings already stabilized in etymology and grammar,"[42] the "meanings miraculously revealed in great literature,"[43] the sciences seeking "linguistic expressions for meanings as yet unexpressed."[44] My experiential past was indeed involved in institutions or structures like the Roman magisterium, regulated ritual like the liturgy, organized lifestyles like the seminary; but not richly enough to include so much that was seen as secular or just non-Roman. Action could hardly escape even my experience; but there was excessive emphasis on the age-old axiom *agere sequitur esse*, "what I do is the consequence, follows from, what or who I am"; not enough emphasis on the contemporary insight (to coin a Latinism) *agere efficit esse*, "what I do is creative of what or who I am." Men and women fashion their future—their own and the world's.

As I struggled to communicate all this to my word processor, I was sharing a remarkable experience on tape. On the evening of July 7, 1990, the three greatest tenors of our time joined forces with an orchestra of two hundred against a majestic background of ancient Rome. In the Baths of Caracalla, on a brilliant starlight night with a full moon rising, before a wildly enthusiastic audience of six thousand, José Carreras, Plácido Domingo, and Luciano Pavarotti, together with Maestro Zubin Mehta, presented an evening of arias, songs, and medleys unique in the annals of recorded music.

Could Ignatius have left his desk in Rome and walked to the Baths of Caracalla, he would have had no difficulty in fitting that evening into his Spiritual Exercises: open your God-given intelligence, open your eyes and your ears, touch and taste and smell—all "to the greater glory of God." Ignatius would agree with two friends of mine, Father Michael Sparough and Betsey Beckman, who have produced audiocassettes that offer moving meditations on our liturgy—on bread and wine, candles and water, oil and the crucifix. The purpose of these meditations? "Open up your senses, so that you can taste, see, hear, smell, and touch God."[45]

M__Y THIRD QUESTION__: Where might you and I insert all this—Ignatian experience of spiritual realities, of our very God—into contemporary Christian living, into your spirituality and mine? Such experience simply must be intimate to our concern for a contemporary spirituality. Recall our broad definition of religious experience: "some sort of awareness of and response to the divine." Now within a genuinely Catholic vision, experience means personal encounter—personal encounter, above all, with a living God. It means, concretely, that you are increasingly sensitive to four phenomenological aspects of your relationship to God in Christ.[46] (1) You find yourself absorbed by a *living* presence, a divine activity more real than your physical surroundings. (2) You are aware of a *holy* presence, that fills you with awe and fear, the while it warms and draws you—what Jean Mouroux called "a kind of rhythm between hope and fear, each mutually supporting and generating the other."[47] (3) You know an inexpressible *loneliness*; for in the presence of Love you are still so far from Love, agonizingly aware that to find yourself you must lose yourself, to grasp God you must risk all. (4) Even within sorrow you sense a profound *joy*, strong and unshakable, a joy that refuses to be imprisoned, must burst forth to be shared with others.

That sort of experience—with its stress on feelings, on emotion, on knowledge in action, on a world present to me not as expressly known but as lived in—clashed with the only really safe experience I knew, the experience that founded Scholastic philosophy and theology. This latter experience was built on cognition: man/woman is essentially a knower. Human perfection is identified with abstract knowledge. It was limited to the experience of making judgments: "Good is to be done, evil avoided." "Artificial contraception is intrinsically evil." "God is; God is all-good, all-powerful, all-just, all-merciful." "Christ is perfect God, perfect man."[48] It was only well into my graying years that I could resonate to Catholic philosopher Jacques Maritain's conviction: The culmination of knowledge is not conceptual but experiential—man/woman "feels" God.[49]

How do you get that way? I begin with a problem that may have occurred to you. Wasn't Ignatius a mystic? And aren't mystics recipients of extraordinary graces, graces not granted to ordinary folk? Specifically, wasn't Ignatius's experience of God the kind of encounter that raised him to a level above the devout but pedestrian Christian, above the Burghardts of this world?

For your consolation, there are mystics and mystics. In a very specialized sense, there are those relatively few mystics who have been gifted by God with an extraordinary grace called infused contemplation, sometimes accompanied by visions, stigmata, levitations, raptures, ecstasies. Such was Teresa of Avila. But over and above these (or, if you prefer, under and below these) you have what is delightfully called "the mysticism of everyday life."[50] This demands explanation.

> *To find yourself you must lose yourself, to grasp God you must risk all.*

Take Thomas Merton, always the contemplative but moving from renunciation to involvement, making contact with Hindu and Buddhist and Sufi, protesting Vietnam and violence, racial injustice and nuclear war. Merton insisted that all Christians are called to the mystical life.[51] Not to its highest flights. But all of us are called to the entire life of prayer—to the experience of emptiness, of purity, of nakedness inseparable from genuine self-giving. Not all can turn to the solitude of monastic life to realize their self-emptying; most, in fact, are called to identify in a special way with the "least" of Jesus' sisters and brothers, with the poor, the despised, the marginalized. This is nothing more nor less than radical fidelity to the demands of daily life—the experience of faith, hope, and love which, the experts tell us, is rooted in all authentic human experiences.

> For example, the experience of utter loneliness; forgiving without expecting reward or even feeling good about one's selflessness; selfless love of others; radical fidelity to one's conscience, even when one appears like a fool before others; being faithful, hopeful, and

loving, even when there are no apparent reasons for so acting; the bitter experience of the wide gulf between what we truly desire and what life actually gives us; a silent hope as one faces death—these and similar experiences are the mysticism of daily life.[52]

Similarly, Jesuit activist William Callahan has focused on what he terms "noisy contemplation."[53] He claims that men and women can and do experience God amid contemporary pressures, today's intense turmoil. It isn't easy. It calls for a heightened awareness of God in us, in others, all around us; it demands that a Christian, like Christ, "be a person who moves in the midst of modern noise and tensions both inside and around us, and who remains aware of others in loving, bonding, and caring ways. . . ."[54] Not that we can dispense with quiet time. I recognize the truth in the old axiom "To work is to pray." But to make work your only prayer is to risk spiritual shipwreck.

Now Ignatius encountered God in ways extraordinary and ordinary. He had a singular experience of the Trinity, encountered God one and three in a fashion indescribable and not the common experience of Christians. And yet, if we can credit Karl Rahner, Ignatius insisted that all Christians are called to encounter God. How does it happen? In ways we tend to overlook.

I encounter God in flashes of inspiration. Listen to thirteenth-century mystic Julian of Norwich as she tells us:

> [God] shewed [me] a little thing, the size of a hazelnut, which seemed to lie in the palm of my hand. . . . I looked upon it with the eye of my understanding, and thought, "What may this be?" I was answered in a general way, thus: "It is all that is made." I wondered how long it could last; for it seemed as though it might suddenly fade away into nothing, it was so small. And I was answered in my understanding: "It lasts, and ever shall last; for God loveth it. And even so hath everything being—by the love of God."
>
> In this little thing I saw three properties. The first is that God made it; the second, that God loveth it; the third, that God keepeth it. And what beheld I in this? Truly, the Maker, the Lover, and the Keeper. . . .[55]

I can encounter God when I experience my own insufficiency, my vulnerability, the radical realization of Jesus' declaration to his disciples, "Apart from me you can do nothing" (Jn 15:5). Not only on the desert sands; not only on a hospital bed, faced with terminal cancer; not only when the prosperity I fashioned falls apart in an economic slump. I experience God when I see myself in my naked reality: my intellect so limited before all there is to know, my senses less keen than those of my long-haired Labrador, the flesh in which I once gloried yielding inexorably to an aging beyond my control, my will witnessing time and again to the truth of St. Paul's anguished confession, "I can will what is right, but I cannot do it" (Rom 7:18).

I can encounter God in the central act of Catholic worship. But only if the Eucharist is central to my day-to-day existence, only if my skin quivers and my bones come alive with the startling, frightening affirmation of God's Son in flesh, "Unless you eat the flesh of the Son of man and drink his blood, you have no life in you" (Jn 6:53).

I can encounter God if I live closer to those whom Christ loved most passionately: the "little ones" of earth, those who fall in varied ways under the heading of "the poor"—the despised and the marginalized, those who hurt often and joy rarely, who share in Christ's crucifixion far more than in his resurrection. For, in Jean Vanier's insight, the poor are prophetic: they have a word of God for us, if we would but listen. "That means staying near them, because they speak quietly and infrequently; they are afraid to speak because they have been broken and oppressed."[56]

I can encounter God if I let go, leap out of my narrow self, let my senses loose to roam this fascinating, bewildering, overwhelming universe, let them discover, with Jesuit poet Gerard Manley Hopkins, that "The world is charged with the grandeur of God"; and even if "All wears man's smudge and shares man's smell,"

> . . . for all this, nature is never spent;
> There lives the dearest freshness deep down things . . .
>   Because the Holy Ghost over the bent
> World broods with warm breast and with ah! bright wings.[57]

In other words, a wondrous way to religious experience, to experience of God, is the contemplation the Carmelite William McNamara defined so deftly, "a long loving look at the real."[58] Not an abstract, intangible God-in-the-sky. Reality is living, pulsing people; fire and ice; a ruddy glass of Burgundy; Beethoven's *Mass in D* and Victor Hugo's *Les misérables*; a child lapping a chocolate ice-cream cone; a striding woman with windblown hair. Reality is the risen Christ. How activate your innate capacity for contemplation? I leave you with five swift suggestions.

1. Some sort of *desert experience*. Not necessarily the physical desert, but an experience that brings you face-to-face with solitude, with vastness, perhaps even with powers of life and death beyond

your control. An experience that evokes your capacity for initiative, interrupts routine patterns and piety, forces you to be alert, recollected, so that issues become clear, reality recognizable. An experience that takes hold of you, turns you inside out, opens the City to contemplation. For in the desert tradition (the Hebrew people, Jesus, the desert fathers) one meaning predominates: The desert is where we encounter God, where God comes to meet God's people: "I will allure her, and bring her into the wilderness, and speak tenderly to her" (Hos 2:14).

> *I can encounter God if I let go, leap out of my narrow self, let my senses loose to roam this fascinating, bewildering, overwhelming universe.*

2. Develop a feeling for *festivity*.[59] I mean activity that is meaningful in itself, not tied to goals, to "so that" or "in order to." It calls for renunciation: you must take usable time and withdraw it from utility. And this you must do out of love, whose expression is joy.

3. Intrinsic to festivity is a sense of *play*. I don't mean "fooling around." I mean what poet Francis Thompson meant when, in his essay on Shelley, he likened the poet's gifts to a child's faculty of make-believe—but raised to the nth power—whose box of toys is the universe, who "makes bright mischief with the moon," in whose hand "the meteors nuzzle their noses." It demands a sense of wonder—a wonder with which we are born, but which most of us lose as we "grow up." Rabbi Abraham Joshua Heschel saw it as our contemporary trap: "believing that everything can be explained, that reality is a simple matter which has only to be organized in order to be mastered. All enigmas can be solved, and all wonder is nothing but 'the effect of novelty upon ignorance.'"[60] No, don't put everything under a microscope, don't program life in a computer. Let your imagination loose to play with ideas—what it means to be alive, to be in love, to believe and to hope.

4. Don't try to *possess* the object of your delight, whether divine or human, imprisoned marble or free-flowing rivulet. Listen to this gem from Walter Kerr:

> To regain some delight in ourselves and in our world, we are forced to abandon, or rather to reverse, an adage. A bird in the hand is

not worth two in the bush—unless one is an ornithologist, the curator of the Museum of Natural History, or one of those Italian vendors who supply restaurants with larks. A bird in the hand is no longer a bird at all: it is a specimen; it may be dinner. Birds are birds only when they are in the bush or on the wing; their worth as birds can be known only at a discreet and generous distance.[61]

5. Read, listen to, make friends with, *remarkable men and women* who have themselves looked long and lovingly at the real. Biblical figures like Abraham and Mary of Nazareth, murmuring "yes" to Yahweh though they knew not where it would take them. Martyrs like twentieth-century Martin Luther King, with a dream of black freedom he bathed in blood. Lao-tzu doing everything through being, Heschel doing everything through worship. Women like Dorothy Day and Mother Teresa, arms embracing the homeless and the hopeless from New York to Calcutta. Short-story writer Flannery O'Connor, dead of lupus at 39, with her mature acceptance of limitation, with her God never far away, quietly loved, with so much Christlife in her frail frame—what I can best describe as grace on crutches. Touch men and women like these, and you will touch the stars—will touch God.

Have I strayed from Ignatian spirituality? Not one whit. Here is Ignatius Loyola not 1491 but 1991. Here is Ignatius declaring to you in a contemporary idiom, "This experience [all of it—experience of God in God's self, in God's things, in God's people] is grace indeed, and basically there is no one to whom it is refused." Reach out for it; reach out for . . . God.

NOTES

[1] Michael J. Buckley, S.J., "Experience and Culture: A Point of Departure for American Atheism," *Theological Studies* 50 (1989): 457.

[2] See W. J. Hill. "Experience, Religious," *New Catholic Encyclopedia*.

[3] Ibid. See further L. Dupré, "Kierkegaard, Søren Aabye," *New Catholic Encyclopedia*.

[4] See J.J. Heaney, "Modernism," *New Catholic Encyclopedia*.

[5] John Courtney Murray, S.J., "The Declaration on Religious Freedom," in *War, Poverty, Freedom: The Christian Response* (Concilium 15; Glen Rock, N.J.: Paulist, 1966), p. 11.

[6] Michael Novak, *The Open Church: Vatican II, Act II* (New York: Macmillan, 1964), p. 67.

[7] My analysis has profited from Raymond Studzinski, O.S.B., "Experience, Religious," *The New Dictionary of Theology*, ed. Joseph A. Komonchak, Mary Collins, and Dermot A. Lane (Wilmington, Del.: Glazier, 1987), pp. 369-74; also from authors he cites: William James, *The Varieties of Religious Experience* [1902] (New York: Collier, 1961); Dermot A. Lane, *The Experience of God* (New York: Paulist, 1981); B. J. Lonergan, "First Lecture: Religious Experience," in *A Third Collection* (Mahwah, N.J.: Paulist, 1985); W. W. Meissner, *Psychoanalysis and Religious Experience* (New Haven: Yale University, 1984); John E. Smith, *Experience and God* (New York: Oxford University, 1968).

[8] Quoted by Paul Elmem, "Death of an Elfking," *Christian Century* 94, no. 37 (Nov. 16, 1977): 1057.

[9] See *The Simone Weil Reader* (New York: David McKay, 1977), p. 12.

[10] See Ashley Montagu, *The Elephant Man: A Study in Human Dignity* (New York: Dutton, 1979), pp. 14-16, 18, 22, 29, 34, 63-64, 77.

[11] Studzinski, "Experience, Religious," p. 369.

[12] Hill, "Experience, Religious."

[13] Here see Denis Edwards, *Human Experience of God* (New York/Ramsey: Paulist, 1983), pp. 1-15.

[14] Ibid, p. 11.

[15] Note Robert Johann's definition of experience: "the dynamic interrelation of the self and the world, grasped, not objectively, but from within, insofar as the self, as self, is present to both itself and the world as co-constituents of an open yet all-inclusive whole" ("Experience and Philosophy," in Irwin C. Lieb, ed., *Experience, Existence, and the Good: Essays in Honor of Paul Weiss* [Carbondale, Ill.: Southern Illinois University, 1961], p. 27).

[16] Alfred North Whitehead, *Adventures of Ideas* (New York: Free Press, 1967), p. 225.

[17] Text from Louis J. Puhl, S.J., *The Spiritual Exercises of St. Ignatius* (Chicago: Loyola University, 1951), p. 50.

[18] See ibid.

[19] Ibid, p. 33.

[20] Ibid.

[21] Ibid.

[22] Ibid, pp. 97-98.

[23] Here I am deeply indebted to Hugo Rahner, S.J., *Ignatius the Theologian* (New York: Herder and Herder, 1968), specifically pp. 181-213, "The Application of the Senses." This chapter is a careful summary of the two schools of thought, a fruitful effort to link the two forms of sense application, and "a short look at the therapeutic value of the Application of the Senses in both its forms" (211). In attempting to simplify a complex issue, I may well have distorted it.

[24] Ibid, pp. 187-88.

[25] See H. Pinard de la Boullaye, "Sentir, sentimiento y sentido dans le style de saint Ignace," *Archivum historicum Societatis Iesu* 25 (1956): 416-30.

[26] Augustine, *Confessions* 10, 6; trans. mine.

[27] Karl Rahner, S.J., *Ignatius of Loyola*, with an Historical Introduction by Paul Imhof, S.J. (London/New York: Collins, 1979), pp. 12-13. I have introduced certain changes in Rosaleen Ockenden's translation, on the basis of the original German edition, *Ignatius von Loyola* (Freiburg i. B.: Herder, 1978), pp. 10-12.

[28] John W. Padberg, S.J., "Personal Experience and the Spiritual Exercises: The Example of Saint Ignatius," *Studies in the Spirituality of Jesuits* 10, no. 5 (November 1978): 263. See *The Autobiography of St. Ignatius Loyola, with Related Documents*, tr. Joseph F. O'Callaghan, ed. John C. Olin (New York: Harper, 1974), p. 28.

[29] *Autobiography*, p. 29.

[30] Ibid.

[31] See ibid.

[32] See ibid, p. 30.

[33] Harvey D. Egan, S.J., *Ignatius Loyola the Mystic* (Wilmington, Del.: Glazier, 1987), p. 43.

[34] See Padberg (n. 18 above), p. 265.

[35] *Autobiography*, p. 30.

[36] Egan, *Ignatius Loyola the Mystic*, p. 44.

[37] *Ignatius von Loyola*, p. 13; trans. mine.

[38] Ibid, p. 13; trans. mostly mine.

[39] Urban T. Holmes III, *Ministry and Imagination* (New York: Seabury, 1976), pp. 97-98. Here Holmes is admittedly borrowing from Owen Barfield, *Saving the Appearances: A Study in Idolatry* (New York: Harcourt, Brace & World, n.d.).

[40] Whitehead, *Adventures of Ideas*, p. 226.

[41] Ibid.

[42] Ibid, p. 227.

[43] Ibid, p. 226.

[44] Ibid, p. 227.

[45] "The Body at Eucharist: Meditations by J. Michael Sparough, S.J., and Betsey Beckman. Music by Bobby Fisher" (Cincinnati: St. Anthony Messenger, 1990), tape 1, side 1.

[46] Here I am indebted to an older but still insightful article by Pierre Fransen, "Towards a Psychology of Divine Grace," *Cross Currents* 8 (1958), specifically pp. 229-30.

[47] Jean Mouroux, *The Christian Experience: An Introduction to a Theology* (New York: Sheed and Ward, 1954), p. 38.

[48] Here I was much influenced by first-rate metaphysician (and no iconoclast) Robert Johann, "Experience and Philosophy," in Lieb, ed., *Experience*, pp. 25-38.

[49] See Jacques Maritain, *The Degrees of Knowledge* (2nd ed.; New York: Scribner, 1938).

[50] Egan calls this "mysticism in the broad sense" (*Ignatius Loyola the Mystic*, p. 21); see discussion ibid, pp. 20-31. On this see also his *Christian Mysticism: The Future of a Tradition* (New York: Pueblo, 1984), esp. pp. 236-37, 246-49.

[51] See Thomas Merton, "Is Mysticism Normal?" *Commonweal* 51 (1949-50): 98.

[52] Egan, *Ignatius Loyola the Mystic*, pp. 21-22.

[53] See William Callahan, S.J., "Noisy Contemplation," in *The Wind Is Rising: Prayer for Active People*, ed. William Callahan, S.J., and Francine Cardman (Mt. Rainier, Md.: Quixote Center, 1978), pp. 34-37.

[54] Ibid, p. 35.

[55] Julian of Norwich, *The Revelations of Divine Love* 5 (*The Revelations of Divine Love of Julian of Norwich*, tr. James Walsh, S.J. [St. Meinrad, Ind.: Abbey, 1974], p. 53).

[56] Jean Vanier, *Community and Growth* (Sydney: St. Paul Publications, 1979), p. 146.

[57] Gerard Manley Hopkins, "God's Grandeur," in *The Poems of Gerard Manley Hopkins*, ed. W.H. Gardner and N.H. MacKenzie (London: Oxford University, 1970), p. 66.

[58] See my article "Contemplation: A Long Loving Look at the Real," *Church* 5, no. 4 (winter 1989): 14-18. In these final paragraphs I am borrowing from a section of this article where the suggestions are developed at greater length.

[59] I recommend Josef Pieper's slender volume *In Tune with the World: A Theory of Festivity* (New York: Harcourt, 1965)—ancient, if you wish, but not dated.

[60] In *Between God and Man: An Interpretation of Judaism from the Writings of Abraham J. Heschel* (New York: Harper, 1959), p. 40.

[61] Walter Kerr, *The Decline of Pleasure* (New York: Simon and Schuster, 1962), p. 48.

Finding a Busy God
David L. Fleming, S.J.

Probably one of the most consistent complaints in our ordinary humdrum lives is that we are too busy. At least it becomes our excuse—for not writing letters, for not making that telephone call, for not being present for that meeting, for not being able to take this day or this weekend off, for not having time to pray.

THE PARADOX OF A BUSY GOD. A paradox is that spiritual traditions—both Christian and non-Christian—are not accustomed to image God as being similarly active as ourselves. Yet ordinarily we human beings make our gods into the kind of images we value. All the strictures against idol-making in the Old Testament represent God's attempt to counter this human inclination to bring God down to the level of our own limited human experience. The struggle persists even for us Christians in every age. For example, through the medieval period and up till Ignatius's time, we were prone to image our God as a medieval king surrounded by his court (this image remains a part of Ignatian spirituality through the *Spiritual Exercises*). A strong image following upon the Council of Trent up to pre-Vatican II times was God as the divine bookkeeper and stern judge (this image still flows from *our* bookkeeping sense in keeping count in our examination of conscience and in confession). Perhaps today for many people God is the divine video game player, removed from the action, an observer God who, to our man-made blips on his heavenly screen, can only react. At the same time some of us, through our yoga exercises or our centering techniques, may feel that the Buddha image represents our God—eternally placid, removed from all the joys and sorrows, toils, and successes and failures, of everyday life—in fact, representing how we may want *this* time of prayer or reflection to be for us.

Why do we have the paradox by which God is ordinarily not imaged with the busyness which we take upon ourselves? It may be that we do not think that it is proper for God to get his hands dirty like our own. Maybe we do not like the competition with our own efforts, so we make sure to keep God in the heavens while we get things done here on earth. More likely we are shaped by our Judeo-Christian traditional account of creation which pictures God resting on the seventh day. In fact, our language about life with God seems to be summed up in the prayer we say for our departed brothers and sisters: "Eternal rest grant unto them, O Lord, and let perpetual light shine upon them."

THE INSIGHT OF IGNATIUS LOYOLA. There is one spiritual tradition which does provide a certain corrective to our image of an eternally resting God. That tradition comes from Ignatius Loyola, who had a certain predilection for describing God, Trinity and Incarnate, as *laboring*. He imaged God as active and Jesus busy about the affairs of this God he called Abba, Father. How does Ignatius come to this imaging of our Christian God and, more importantly for us, how does it affect the way we live—with ourselves, our God, and our world?

In order to find our way in answering these questions, let us take a closer look at the man Ignatius Loyola. The most revealing image which Ignatius uses to describe himself is captured in the word "pilgrim"—which he does in the book identified as his *Autobiography*. Why the choice of this word pilgrim? Who is a pilgrim? A pilgrim is one on the move, an active person, one who is not wandering aimlessly but has a purpose and a direction, one whose place of origin (where he or she comes from) is less important than the destination of one's journey (where one is going). A pilgrim expands natural affections for family and friends to his or her fellow travelers. "We"—all of us travelers—share and grow in our identity as pilgrims *together*, and this identity coming from activity and mission becomes the most important reality for our relationship with God. "Pilgrims together" become the People of God. For Ignatius and his early band of followers, "pilgrims together" became companions of Christ, the Company of Jesus.

Ignatius prided himself on being a pilgrim up to the moment of his death in July 1556. But he did not think of himself as starting that way. Not uncommon for many of us in our own human stories, there was a sense in the younger Ignatius of what he thought his life should be about. He wanted an education, a successful life of "making it" by knowing the right people and associating with them and by living in the right places. He wanted people to notice him for what he did, and he wanted the good life.

The primary experience of Ignatius is not his doing great things for God, but God actively entering into his life.

War—actually a rather futile defense of the Spanish city of Pamplona against French forces—dramatically changed Ignatius's life-goals. Although Ignatius's life would be changed and his life as a pilgrim undertaken, we need to recognize that any conversion moment has to build on our human personality, with its emotions and affections, its education and understanding, its desires and dreams. In this conversion moment for Ignatius, to do great things was still deep in his makeup, only now "to do great things" focused on God ("just like St. Francis or St. Dominic did," so Ignatius wrote, *Autobiography*, 7). But the primary experience of Ignatius is rather not his doing great things for God, but God actively entering into his life, "teaching him like a schoolboy" (he was thirtysomething) and setting a new direction for his life.

Ignatius the mystic, unlike Teresa of Avila and John of the Cross, does not find himself called to rest in the ecstasy of a union of love. The mystical experience of Ignatius, which becomes a part of this conversion moment, does not give him so much visions to gaze upon or moments of intimacy to savor, but insight into the *workings* of God's mysteries. He was given to understand God's *working* in creation; he was given to understand Jesus' active presence in the Eucharist; he was given to understand how all things work together, both spiritual and material. In fact, he was given so much understanding in one particular enlightening experience that at age sixty-two, thirty years after this conversion, he says "if he were to gather all the helps he had received from God and everything he knew and add them together, he does not think that they would equal all that he received at that one time" (*Autobiography*, 30).

These mystical experiences happening early on in this conversion time of Ignatius's life appear to fix his relationship to a God who actively seeks our collaboration in laboring. The rest of his pilgrim life was spent in working out for himself and for others the maintenance and development of this relationship to a busy God. Probably many of us are more familiar with the traditional Ignatian slogan "finding God in all things." What is not apparent in that phrasing is the importance of the *kind* of God we seek.

THE IGNATIAN MOVEMENT IN FINDING GOD. How does Ignatius try to communicate his understanding of union through activity to those of us who have not shared a mystical experience like his? We all can acknowledge at certain times in our lives the lack of any feeling for the presence of God; this can especially happen when we get caught up in the many things we have to do. For Ignatius this common human experience points to the basic human need and appreciation for what he identifies as the grace of devotion. God wants to enter into our lives easily; from our perspective—*our* ease in finding God—this is the grace of devotion. We all are meant to be people of devotion. Devotion defined as ease in finding God is the necessary antidote to a spiritual life which is described as "dried up" or a life "too busy for spiritual things." From the Ignatian perspective, Christians are meant to live life with devotion, with an ease in finding God.

Of course, our ease in finding God is related to the places where we need to seek and find God's presence. Here lies the importance of the Ignatian imaging of God. Although I know of no direct Ignatian quotation of the passage, in the gospel of St. John (5:17) the words "My Father is working still, and I am working" capture the prevailing God-picture in Ignatian spirituality. For example, within his *Spiritual Exercises*, in suggesting the context of the Incarnation, Ignatius looks to a trinitarian God coming to the decision: "Let us *work* the redemption of the human race" (SpEx 107). In his consideration of the Nativity, Ignatius sees Mary and Joseph "journeying and *laboring*" (SpEx 116), only to bring Jesus into the world so that, after many *labors*, he may die on the cross. Ignatius repeats this way of considering Jesus' life during his consideration of the gospel mysteries dealing with the Passion when he suggests that we frequently bring to mind the *labors*, fatigues, and pains of Jesus from the moment when he was born up to the present mystery which we are contemplating (SpEx 206). Even with the Resurrection, Ignatius pictures Jesus as bearing the office of consoler (SpEx 224)—doing the *work* of strengthening his brothers and sisters. And, of course, the call of Christ goes out to each person to come join with him, so that through laboring together they may also follow him in glory (SpEx 95).

God wants to enter into our lives easily.

Where, then, do we begin to look for God? In activity, in laboring. But what distinguishes Ignatius's outlook is not our crying out for God to be with us in *our* labors, but rather envisioning that we are privileged to join God in God's activities, in God's laborings. More correctly viewed, we are always meant to be working *with God* and with God's world. Our union with God, with Christ, is primarily found, then, in activity conjoined with God, with Christ.

How is this way of acting to come about? How do we enter the process of finding a busy God? Ignatius nowhere sets down a concise "how to," but the pattern becomes clear in his own life story, in his writings, in his letters of counsel. Our union builds upon a four-step movement similar to the graced movement through the Weeks of the Ignatian Exercises. We need to remember that the movement is *one*—a single movement, even though repeated innumerable times in the course of our human lives and even though we experience discrete and distinct steps within it. Let us describe the distinct steps within this one movement of devotion, our growing ease in finding a busy God.

THE FIRST STEP. The first step is recognition or awareness of God as busy, the God who acts, the One who labors for me, for us; our response to One so actively working for our well-being is gratitude. For Ignatius, there is always a response to the question "What can I (or we) do for God?" Before such a laboring God, the first response of us humans, the most basic response is "to give thanks." So far this may sound all too easy—the discovery of a new awareness of God, a busy God, totally engaged in the workings of our world, and as a result the immediacy of our response of gratitude. But each step retains its own peril. Far too often the peril of this first step lies in its ordinariness, its encircling commonplace. Who does not forget to give thanks for something or someone that is always there? Or perhaps expressing gratitude all too quickly, we leave it only in words—words tending to have less and less real meaning. What can we do? Ignatius encourages us to allow, daily, this basic imaging of an active God and our response of gratitude to permeate us by means of our own conscious and deliberate exercising. Two practices become part of his schema for growth in devotion, in our ease in finding a busy God.

> One cannot practice detachment until one has a felt experience of attachment.

The first practice is the daily examination of conscience or, as we commonly say today, the examination of consciousness. Gratitude and our regular assessing of the presence or absence of God in our daily activities and events are central to this reflective practice.

The second practice that Ignatius proposes is perhaps even more helpful for this first step toward greater devotion. In fact, only in the context of a laboring God do we gain insight into the centrality of Eucharist in Ignatian spirituality. Eucharist remains central to Ignatian spirituality, not out of medieval piety, but out of mystical vision. Eucharist expresses our most basic relationship to God in two moments—a response first in giving thanks to God for all God's activity and especially God's activity in, through, and with Christ and then in handing over to God our own efforts to continue the one saving action begun in Christ and continued now through our own collaboration. Eucharist is at one and the same time a celebration of ongoing love and of ongoing work. In a similar conjoining of notions, at the close of the *Spiritual Exercises,* Ignatius points out that love ought to be put more in deeds than in words (SpEx 230). Both understandings point to the identifying of union with activity.

THE SECOND STEP. A second step which occurs naturally in this movement is the actual giving of ourselves over to the activity or work at hand. The peril for this step comes from two extreme reactions: (1) being afraid to invest ourselves in an activity or keeping a distance by performing only out of obligation or (2) so investing ourselves that we become the "owners" of the activity or work, leaving to God little or no place. For Ignatius, activity reveals how God acts in us and in creation. Yet *our* very activity can cause us to focus on our own efforts and begin to close us in on our own accomplishments or successes. Ignatius's warnings to young Jesuits in studies about the drying up of their devotion are just as much in terms of this temptation as in the temptation of trying to recapture their previous moments of devotion in more prayer. What Ignatius draws our attention to is that even those works undertaken for the love of God—in fact, even prayer itself—easily become the occasion of a self-focusing or self-centering. This shift to a self-focus happens all too often to those who try to practice an active or apostolic spirituality—even to the people who have been inspired by Ignatius.

Ignatius's approach is wise and spiritually sound. One cannot practice detachment until one has a felt experience of attachment. We cannot pretend beforehand to disengage ourselves from investment in our works so that a sense of selfishness or ownership will not take hold. We would be guilty of a certain naïveté, as if we were for a time free from being sinners and free from the necessity of being saved. Our very activity leads us necessarily to a redemptive moment—redemptive in that it focuses our eyes on the crucified Christ and redemptive in that it calls us to our own dying. We have begun the third step.

THE THIRD STEP. The third step of the movement deals with sacrifice. What is the cost of this activity or work to the self? What are we willing to pay? Ignatius expressed the principle in this fashion: Our activity in Christ will advance in proportion to the surrender of our own self-love and of our own will and interests (SpEx 189). Ignatius knew that the very activity in which we engage will necessarily call for a dying to self. He uses terms which are no longer common in our spirituality vocabulary—*abnegation* and *mortification*. Abnegation and mortification hardly seem to suggest growth and development, and in our Christian spiritual tradition, we may have invoked these words too readily to squelch the normal and necessary development of personality and freedom. Perhaps that is why the peril involved in this third step seems to be the most formidable. A denying of self, a dying to self is demanded of our every activity if we are to remain collaborators with God. But it is not for us to name the day or the hour. This radical dying to self is spread over a lifetime. As we grow in our sense of detachment and freedom, we may find our hands less clutching, but a certain pain of loss remains with every small dying. We find ourselves allied with Christ in the struggle of handing over even the activity of dying itself: "Father, into your hands, we commend our spirit."

We do not so much do good things for others as allow God's love to touch others through the God who has touched us.

Besides the fact that it is not for us to determine the *times* of our self-denial or our dying, we also find ourselves powerless to determine the *kind* of denial or dying which will be demanded of us. We may more likely discover a rhythm or pattern of dyings which *each activity or work determines and we do not*. For example, self-denial or dying may occur as tedium in a necessary activity to be done. Perhaps it is the hiddenness or taken-for-granted character of our work that demands our dying to self. Maybe the dying comes in our always being sent on by someone who has authority over us and never seeing a work through to its completion. There is a kind of dying in the pain of separation from coworkers we love and in the self-denying pain of working with those difficult and disagreeable people who may come with the job. Without this kind of *self*-denying, we deny a place to an active God; we become the possessors, the occupiers of our very works, and we settle in, breaking our pilgrim stride.

Ignatius the pilgrim leads us all along a path which is very dangerous because every created reality can and likely will become the occasion of this interior struggle of denial and dying to self. And yet the one who is afraid of giving oneself over to work or activity holds back from losing self to find God. Such a one mistrusts the God who forever is working to save. The temptation to leave off from an activity once begun because of a possible over-self-involvement must be faced, according to Ignatius, by the stance that "the love and service of God our Lord" was our purpose in beginning *this* work and it remains our purpose in seeing it through. So our very seeking union with God through activity becomes an inexhaustible source of self-denial and dying to self.

T HE FOURTH STEP. The fourth step in our movement we might describe as a conversion of love. The love which allows us to turn our gaze upon a God who is so actively engaging, a Love that draws forth our sense of gratitude, becomes a love that moves us to be with God in whatever the task we are given or that we take on. But then comes the inevitable testing and trial time of our activity, and the love with which we love what we do (the work with all its circumstances of people and places) is being smelted free of the slag of our own self-will. Through our effort to seek and find a busy God, our love is always being changed into purer apostolic love. If in the Ignatian vision everything is prayer, the reason is that love and activity now grow together. This is the necessary conversion of Christian love.

What is the peril in this fourth step? The peril lies in a reluctance to go back to step one over and over again, but the grace of devotion—our ease in finding God—nourishes our prayer and commands our activity. Our works uniting us to our busy God allow us to extend that graced love to our neighbor. We do not so much do good things for others as allow God's love to touch others through the God who has touched us.

P RAYER AND WORK. For Ignatius, the prayer of contemplating the Trinity *working* the salvation of humankind is a distinct graced moment which is all of a piece and fused with the graced moment of the work of our own finding God wherever or in whatever we are engaged. Prayer and work are distinct activities and yet interrelate and become fused in a way similar to the redemptive work of Christ, distinctive and yet fused with the creative work of the Word of God (Ignatius addresses *Jesus as our Creator* hanging on the cross, in the First Week of the *Spiritual Exercises*, 53). Both the work of creation and the work of redemption form a history in which the Three Persons—Father, Son, and Spirit—work in concert and in which they ask us to collaborate. So, too, the activity of prayer and the activity of work are meant to be in concert in our relationship with God.

Ignatius's gift to us in our own day is still to point the way for our own pilgrim life of movement and activity. In our prayer and contemplation we meet a busy God, and it is then that we begin to find with greater ease this very God in all our activity. For the work which we do with our hands and our heads is meant always to bring us more fully into that divine history we contemplate—the only history there is, apart from hell.

Finding a busy God provides an incentive to our work because we discover that the very labor which characterizes us as human is a special place where God is. So much needs to be done, and God calls us to the task of building with him a world at once more human and more divine. At the same time, finding a busy God provides us with a way to free ourselves from useless anxiety and impatience about accomplishing any one work according to *our* time schedule. As necessary as God has made us to his busyness, we still remain only collaborators. Every time we pray as Jesus taught us, we speak out our faith in the divinely assured coming of that kingdom. "Thy Kingdom come," we pray. For that hope we work; in that divine assurance we relax.

A FINAL REFLECTION. To return to where we began. We humans all too often feel *guilty* about our busyness, especially in our relationship with God. It is true that busyness can betray a totally pagan approach to our personal value (defined only in terms of what we *do*), to our world (defined as *ours*), and to our God (imaged as a bystander). But by taking cognizance of the busyness of God, as evidenced in the images used by Jesus which our gospels provide and in Jesus' own actions, we find ourselves working hand in glove with him. We are, after all, created in the image and likeness of God—then how is it we are so caught up in activity if activity is not an image of God? If busy we must be, then let us thereby find our God.

Let Ignatius have the last words to send us forth. He writes in one of his letters of counsel: "I have no doubt that your holy intention and direction will make *spiritual* and very acceptable to his Infinite Goodness all that is keeping you busy to God's glory."

Christian Responsibility for Today's World

Monika K. Hellwig

THE SAINTS OF OUR TRADITION have contributed to a precious heritage handed down to us generation after generation, each contributing characteristic insights and inspirations. Generally they have left us with the example of their lives, often with teachings and reflections which they themselves or others have committed to writing, sometimes with structured communities that carry on their work and way of life, and always with a wider and more pervasive influence which is invisible and almost impossible to trace because it has already been absorbed and assimilated into the life of the Church. Ignatius left us all four, but I shall concentrate on the second, because his life is well known, because the Jesuit community can speak for itself, and because the assimilated influence is matter only for speculation. Also, I looked at the lineup of speakers and saw that I was the only lay speaker in the group and decided immediately that I should address very specifically the Ignatian tradition as a resource for *lay* Christian life.

Ignatius left a good deal in writing: a great many letters, documents pertaining to the Society of Jesus, precious autobiographical sketches, and his *Spiritual Exercises*. It is this last which is most clearly constitutive of Ignatian spirituality as a gift to lay Christians in all walks of life. It is, however, committed to posterity in a unique and curious form—a kind of rough map for a journey. Like any map, it does not fill in the content of the landscape, nor does it even indicate the exact route to be traveled like the green line on a AAA Triptik. Each traveler makes a unique, though guided, journey. This, I believe, is one of the main reasons why the legacy of Ignatian spirituality is so apt for the Christian formation of laypeople in our times. There are many parallels between Ignatius's time and our own: the confusion of values in public and private life; the babble of strident voices offering conflicting advice; the need to adapt to a very different role of the Church in the society at large; the need to rethink a synthetic view of Christian beliefs in the light of new learning—in his day the outcome of the Renaissance, in our day the impact of the natural sciences with massive technology at their command. At such times it is not possible to give the believer blueprints and chalk lines. What each believer needs is, rather, strong anchorage in well-thought-out and fully appropriated convictions, a clear sense of the ultimate goal which will act like a compass to set the direction, and a well-formed habit of discernment to deal with the unexpected and the unprecedented which have become common experiences for all of us.

> *It is not possible to give the believer blueprints and chalk lines.*

There is, however, another reason for the curiously apt character of Ignatian spirituality as shaped by the *Spiritual Exercises* for lay Christian life in our times. This second reason, it seems to me, rests on the dissimilarity of Ignatius's time to our own. The guidance provided by the *Exercises* is not based on some original insight or idea; it is profoundly and pervasively biblical and traditional. Living when he did, Ignatius still had the experience of Christendom—the integration of faith with secular life which leaves no margin of the profane; the shaping of imagination and vision by an exuberance of interrelated religious imagery everywhere; the easy sense of belonging and owning the tradition; an awareness of living in the presence of God that was constantly inculcated by the environment even in the midst of the lustiest sinning. In Ignatius's time all this was already threatened with dissolution, but he had known such a life context, and its riches inform the thought and inspiration he passed on. Few of us in our generation have experienced even momentary glimpses of Christendom, and our religious sense is much impoverished by that.

The *Exercises* offer a remarkable blend: they shape the imagination with treasures of the tradition and they form the individual to stand by personal conviction and to walk by well-grounded discernment.

Five characteristics of Ignatian spirituality offer a particularly strong foundation for accepting and exercising Christian responsibility in and for today's world. The spirituality called forth by the *Exercises* is a spirituality of gratitude and reverence, of critical awareness, of empowerment and responsibility, of action, and it is a revolutionary spirituality. I shall comment on each of these aspects and its relevance and value for Christian lay life in our time—especially for our responsibility in shaping today's world with all its human problems and challenges, large and small.

A SPIRITUALITY OF GRATITUDE AND REVERENCE. In the *Exercises* the theme of gratitude and reverence is sounded at the outset in the Principle and Foundation, and comes finally to the fullest orchestration in the Contemplation to Attain Divine Love. No one who has deeply reflected on what is proposed in those brief texts, and allowed them to resonate in the imagination and the affections, could be existentially unaware that "the earth is the Lord's, and the fullness thereof, the world and all those who dwell therein." In Jewish tradition, when Moshe ben Maimon, the great medieval scholar, was asked, "Do you have to treat converts the same as born Jews?" he said, "Yes, of course you do, according to the law." But then he thought about it some more and said, "Yes, you have to treat them the same way, but their experience is never really quite the same because, if you are born and raised a Jew, you feel God like the ground under your feet." The aim in the Ignatian tradition is similar. Formation that begins with deep reflection on gratitude and on dependence, with a view to the acquisition of reverence, is an attempt to bring people whose culture inhibits them from feeling God as the ground under their feet to the point where they do feel God like the ground under their feet.

Such reflection leaves a sense that all is gift, that the gift is good, and that respect, reverence, and stewardship are due to all created things and, beyond this, that overwhelming gratitude is due to their source and maker.

That matter of bonding, of belonging—of feeling secure and therefore having a basis for great courage and the ability to undertake risks—is tied with something that has been rediscovered about Ignatian spirituality and about the Exercises, namely, the extent to which they appeal to affectivity, the extent to which they encourage the person in the process of formation and no doubt for the rest of life to feel the nearness of God, to feel gratitude, to feel, for that matter, sorrow.

Such a foundation of gratitude and reverence is necessary to Christian spirituality at any time. In an intensified way it is necessary in our time because high technology, generally available, gives a sense of independence which isolates and because that same technology puts into our hands an awesome degree of power which can be used humanely and constructively but can also be abused. Because of the isolating sense of independence, there is little sense of gratitude, or of being beholden to anyone. Entertainment media convey to young people a view of society which suggests they owe nothing to parents, educators, or others who spend themselves on their behalf. Popular psychology encourages people to focus on self-fulfillment, acknowledging business arrangements but not personal bonds of obligation. In ordinary psychological reflection on human development, it is often said that without good bonding in childhood it is very difficult to allow one's affectivity to develop, to be fruitful and constructive. We have a tradition that goes right to the Scriptures. Ignatius did not invent it; his tradition gave it to him, a tradition drawn from the Scriptures as interpreted all through the centuries by many saints and many pious customs: the development of an affection for God, a strong bond through emotion, through feeling.

Today interdependence among persons is not stressed, and the human community's dependence on the care and preservation of the gifts of creation tends to receive lip service only, taking second place to instant private profit. Authentic stewardship of the resources of the earth on behalf of all—the poor and powerless and marginated as well as the people of the future—emerges from the sense that all is gift, all is held in trust from the source and maker, who can call for strict accounting, but who invites a grateful and generous response that obviates the necessity of strict accounting.

A SPIRITUALITY OF CRITICAL CONSCIOUSNESS. St. Anselm long ago defined theology as faith seeking understanding. When it seeks understanding, faith becomes stronger, more practical, more viable. I find this characteristic in Ignatian spirituality, partly because the way of formation or reflection that is based on the *Spiritual Exercises* of Ignatius moves immediately from the foundation of gratitude, of bonding, to the question of sin. Ignatian spirituality as represented in the *Spiritual Exercises* appears to be heavily dependent on radical repentance. This is not readily appreciated in our times. We are taught to look for mental health by cultivating a positive outlook, avoiding entrapment in guilt feelings, and being careful not to impose guilt feelings on others. This has left many contemporary Christians bewildered in dealing with a traditional emphasis on sin and repentance in Christian faith and practice. Many questions arise from the contemporary ethos of "I'm OK, you're OK," and many more with its common variant "I'm OK, you're not so hot." Both are uncritical stances which break down very quickly in actual experience. However, we may also have to consider whether our understanding of the traditional notions of sin and repentance is inadequate in the light of experience.

> *Authentic stewardship emerges from the sense that all is gift, all is held in trust from the source and maker.*

One of the problems about a culture that does not have room for examination of consciousness and for repentance is that its imagination becomes stunted. Such a culture lets you think that the way things are is inevitable; it lets you think that of course we have racism, of course we have poverty, of course we have injustices, of course we have wars, of course we devote our resources to manufacturing weapons when there are people starving. In the face of such fatalism or pessimism, repentance is in fact a very optimistic message, for it suggests that things can be different. Only if our attention is focused on repentance or the possibility of repentance can we take a critical view about what is going on, knowing that it is not inevitable, that it could be other than it is.

In the early Church a sense of what sin meant was acquired by reflecting on the difference in one's own life before and after baptism into the Christian community, and by reflecting on the difference in culture and social relations between society at large and the Christian community. From this observation and reflection, sin was implicitly defined in terms of a state of affairs rather than specific actions, in terms of a disorientation of values, expectations, and relationships. The "sin of Adam," which we later came to call original sin, loomed large as a critical tool for judging what was right and what was wrong in human life, society, and behavior. Specific actions were known to be indicative of underlying order or disorder.

The initial Ignatian meditations on sin, though they certainly could be used to spread an ethos of gloom and self-condemnation, lend themselves readily to the cultivation of critical consciousness about one's individual life and about our society. Reflection on the "sin of the angels," the "sin of Adam," and any single decisive sin lends itself, especially in the light of modern scripture scholarship, to a liberation of critical consciousness about what is going on in our world. The doctrine of sin is, at root, an optimistic one because it implies that the way things are in the world is not the way the Creator intends them to be and that a bold and radical transformation and enhancement of human life is possible. Reflection on sin (not simply an unthinking acknowledgment of it) means using the imagination to reassemble the elements of experience in order to discern how it might be quite otherwise in our world in response to God's invitation.

The doctrine of sin is optimistic because it implies that the way things are in the world is not the way the Creator intends them to be.

The focus, then, in the Ignatian tradition, on moving to an understanding of the redemption from first confronting sinfulness is really a way of educating the imagination to be critical, educating people to look at the world with critical consciousness, not simply assimilating what is there but asking what ought to be there and why it is not; asking, when there is unnecessary suffering, what caused it, where is it coming from. Asking why, if there is confusion, despair, frustration. What is it that is out of gear? And all these questions, of course, derive their optimism from what I mentioned before, namely, a deep sense of bonding with a creator God who gives good gifts, gifts that can work.

Such seems to be the intent of Ignatius, rooted in the earliest and most central traditions of the Christian community. It is not strange, therefore, that the liberation theologies of our time have often emerged through the pastoral and theological mediation of those formed in this tradition of spirituality. The meditations on sin at the beginning of the formative "exercises" are not set aside in order to reflect on redemption, grace, and virtue, but lead to the later crucial meditations on the Call of the King and the Two Standards.

A SPIRITUALITY OF EMPOWERMENT AND RESPONSIBILITY. What happens in these two famous meditations is that the issues of sin and grace are placed in the dynamic context of the human community in history. No one makes choices for or against God in a vacuum or in a neutral environment. The redemption is a pervasive, conflictual, and interpersonal process; those who are not with Jesus as redeemer are, quite literally, against him by impeding the process. The redemption is, in the basic sense of the word, a revolutionary process because it aims at radical changes in all aspects of human life, behavior, and relationships. To ally oneself with Christ means to take a countercultural stance, a critical and responsible stance.

While it is commonly accepted among Christians that life involves a struggle against temptations to sin and that the grace of Christ empowers the followers of Jesus to conduct that struggle successfully, there seems to be in Ignatian spirituality a sharper, clearer emphasis both on the empowerment and on the responsibility. In the early Church any account of what Jesus had done for his followers focused on two related aspects: enlightenment and empowerment. By his friendship, his example, and his teaching, Jesus had thrown light on the true meaning and possibilities of their lives. By constant reflection on his attitudes, his way of handling things, his way of making decisions, these early Christians expected to see more and more clearly what life was meant to be and how they might change it; and, by seeing more clearly and experiencing their own link with Jesus, they felt themselves empowered to act creatively and redemptively far beyond what they had thought they could do.

Much the same sense of call and context is to be found in the outlook and spirituality of Ignatius as handed on in the legacy of his famous retreat notes. The retreatant is invited to go to the source, to the life and teachings of Jesus himself, in order to be both enlightened and empowered. It is a matter of learning discipleship, of finding out what Jesus is sending each to do, and of entering into the heat of the action. Indeed, Ignatius does not hesitate to write of a campaign and of Jesus as commander-in-chief and strategist. Yet it is clear that there is a present dynamic involved; it is not a strategy thought out long ago, culminating in elaborate Church structures and carefully laid-out patterns for behavior and worship. There is more at stake than that; there is a call for discernment on the part of each follower and for response to experienced reality, not only obedience to existing rules or the following of preordained patterns.

A SPIRITUALITY OF ACTION. Ignatius was a contemplative in action. His notes and letters suggest that he saw this as the norm for Christian life once an initial formative period was over. Serious discipleship is expected to lead to solidly consequential decisions, establishing an appropriate direction and mode of life, involving a full commitment of personal and material resources, and resulting in the elimination of what might be called the profane margins of one's life. Perhaps this last phrase calls for clarification. What has to be eliminated is not action in the world, but attitudes, expectations, and values which explicitly or implicitly place the political, economic, cultural, recreational or any other aspects of human experience outside the realm of a Christian commitment as though irrelevant to the redemption.

Ignatian tradition, it seems to me, proposes that what ought to come out of prayer, from meditating on the public life of Jesus, is a wholehearted understanding of the discipleship that is called forth from us. During the lifetime of Ignatius that would still have meant to many people a responsible conduct of the duties of their "state in life." Therefore, in the text of the *Spiritual Exercises*, there is heavy emphasis on the personal disposition of readiness to respond to God's call in the choosing of a state of life. This emphasis, however, is balanced by the observation that some may make the Exercises when they no longer have this choice to make, but have some significant issues to face within their present state of life. In our day this second category of significant choices has opened up into a daunting plurality of possibilities and options. Democracy, social mobility, patterns of employment, possibilities of midlife career changes, and women's opportunities to combine careers with families, to mention just a few, are all changes that call for wise choices daily, even hourly, and for an authentic commitment of one's resources to collaboration with Christ in the redemption.

The criteria for discernment which Ignatius proposes as suitable for the choice of a way of life, and the mode he suggests for attaining the proper disposition, are for the lay Christian today not something that might provide an occasional critical resource, but something that is required as daily equipment. Many reasons account for this. Social, economic, and cultural change is greatly accelerated in our times, constantly presenting new situations. In contemporary democracies political responsibility, in the broad sense of shaping the structures and functioning of society, now rests with all of us. The general permissiveness of society at large and its unwillingness to impose basic moral norms or to censor and regulate itself, leaves many ambiguous and ambivalent situations which call for the utmost dedication and discernment from each of us. There is so little we can take for granted, so little we can assume the society has predetermined and regulated rightly, justly, for authentic human life and for the common good. So much around us calls for vigorous action that must spring from individual initiative if it is to happen at all. We cannot fulfill our Christian commitment by passively floating along with the tide of affairs in city, state, country, continent, or world.

A REVOLUTIONARY SPIRITUALITY. The Ignatian tradition of spirituality is strongly marked by its eschatological perspective. That is to say, it does not function timelessly but with reference to history and to a Christian vision of the goals and tasks of history. Though the language used about the king and the campaign has the colorful character of sixteenth-century Spain and Portugal in their colonial expansion as seen through the eyes of a Basque, the basic idea of the goal toward which all Christian action must tend is biblical, namely, the realization of the reign of God in all human affairs. Such a goal implies radical change in human relationships, structures of society, values and expectations, and all aspects of behavior and experience.

To many Christians of our times, the notion that Christian faith demands a countercultural lifestyle and radical action for social justice and peace seems ludicrous because they see themselves as living in an essentially Christian country and culture. We have become accustomed to the idea that living by faith is a matter of maintaining values and patterns already established. In his own lifetime Ignatius saw that it could not be so because too much that was taken for granted as part of a Christian culture was corrupt and corrupting. Yet Ignatius testifies that in his early life this was not apparent to him. It was only after his radical conversion process, in which the pattern and idea of the *Spiritual Exercises* were formed, that he began to look at his own society with systematically critical Christian eyes and to live in a very unconventional and prophetic way. Those who follow the pattern of his meditations today are liable to the same kind of Christian eye-opening illumination by the light of the Gospel, and our society is in greater need of such visionary and prophetic critique and action than was the society of the sixteenth century.

Love is appropriately expressed in deeds. We do not imagine the love of a married couple as consisting simply of telling each other that they love each other; we do not imagine that parental love is fulfilled by parents repeatedly telling their children that they love them. There are bumper stickers that ask: "Have you hugged your kid today?" "Did you tell somebody you love them?" Obviously those questions touch on something important, but we know that, essentially, love is in action, is in commitment, and that commitment involves resources, material resources, intellectual resources, contacts, power, access to decision making—all of that and more.

An extraordinarily helpful thing in the Ignatian tradition is that it brings to the fore the necessity of eliminating the profane margins of our lives. What I mean by that—profane, of course, in the literal sense means outside the temple, outside the sacred—is that surely in all of history, in every religious tradition including Christianity, people, because of a certain lethargy, tend to narrow down their faith commitment to ritual-worship activities and to some limited observance of rules. Jesus reminded people that they do not establish God's reign by saying "Lord, Lord," but by doing the will of God, by noticing and taking care of the needs of others.

It is true that the action which Ignatius initiated and inspired in his own times was, for the most part, not directly political or based on systemic or structural critique, but then he did not live in a democratic society with modern communications, mass media, extensive means of economic and social analysis and engineering, and ever more ways of technically transforming human life and livelihood. For ourselves, who live in this type of society, the revolutionary imperative of the Ignatian approach to the meaning of human life and to the responsibilities of being a Christian becomes constantly clearer and more urgent.

It is a revolutionary imperative, not in the sense of calling for violent overthrow of governments, of course, but as regards the need for a far-reaching and foundational assessment of our society in the light of the divine purpose as best we can discern it, and then for appropriate action in all our choices and all our relationships and attitudes and expectations.

Such appropriate action is action not simply within the Church, not simply within the ritual aspects of our lives, the observances, the worship. It involves the totality of our lives, not only our private lives. It involves the way we structure our society. Such action in society is certainly what was understood and envisioned by the earliest Christians in their small and quite unconventional societies. It is characteristic of Ignatian spirituality to assume that this task of transformation was not completed at any time in the past, but continues to be the task of Christians.

Traditionally we have tended to use the word "vocation" for people who are called to be priests, people who are called to be religious, but the advice in the *Spiritual Exercises* about the choice of a way of life applies in our time to choices lay Christians have to make almost every day. We have a great many options, and we need criteria by which to choose among those options and manage our lives. Many challenges come face-to-face with our value system. New situations call for constant discernment, a habit of discernment, which in our day we have to cultivate to be Christians at all. There is a whole tradition of guidance about how to reflect on and properly make those kinds of choices. That seems to be one of the things Jesus was most concerned about. Remember his compassion for the multitudes who ran around like sheep without a shepherd, not knowing why they exist or what they are supposed to be doing. In our time we are not going to get blueprints or chalk lines. We need deep understanding of where our roots are, of what we are called to, and what criteria to use in making our judgments.

Ignatian spirituality is, indeed, a revolutionary spirituality. It asks not only for action but for a particular kind of action. Before Vatican II people spoke a lot about fulfilling the duties of one's state in life. The usual understanding behind those words was that people had their slots, that society was functioning more or less correctly, and that all one had to do to be good was to do fill one's slot and do the right thing within it.

We thought of the Church in much the same way. We tended to see the Church as a maintenance operation. It had been constituted to do its job and was doing it. We were to be in it, to participate in its sacramental life, to follow the rules, and to remain unspotted by this world in not quite the sense that was meant in the New Testament. But with Vatican II we discovered that we are not in a world where the Church could afford to be a maintenance operation. It had to be instrumental for something else, to collaborate in the redemption of the world. It had to be instrumental in welcoming the reign of God into all aspects of human life. That does not mean that people get blueprints and chalk lines for the purpose; it means that they have to have discernment, that they have to have imagination, that they have to have the courage to take risks, that they have to be able to make mistakes, that they have to imagine the world quite differently, that they have to consistently ask not only what is happening but also what should be happening and what it takes to make it happen.

> *We discovered that we are not in a world where the Church could afford to be a maintenance operation.*

For these reasons we badly need the kind of formation that traditional Ignatian spirituality has to offer to our day when we are rediscovering the dynamic of our faith: the call to go beyond mere safety and transform the world.

Vatican II's *Lumen Gentium* says that the Church could be at any time a small number; *pusillus grex* is the term used, "little flock," but that would not be a problem if it is doing what it is supposed to be doing, which is to be the *light of the nations*—the very name of the document. What it is supposed to do is to be a sign and a means of unity and of hope and therefore a rescue for the whole human community.

The Church is rediscovering its own vocation, and within the Church's rediscovery we have to rediscover our own vocation. We rediscover it every day because it is not something that is all set beforehand; it is possibilities opening out step-by-step as we go. It is based, of course, on realizing, from our prayer and from our commitment, that radical change is really possible; and in the *Spiritual Exercises* it is based very much on the meditations on the Passion and Resurrection, the great breakthrough.

The characteristic accompaniment of the great breakthrough is the tremendous dynamic of hope. Shortly before the time of Jesus, the scribes would say: We cannot tell you what the coming reign of God is like, but we can tell you the way to find out. Live now as though God reigned and nobody else has any power or any say-so. If you do that, you will likely be persecuted. If you are not out-and-out persecuted, at least people will take advantage of you. If they do not seriously take advantage of you, at least they will ridicule you and say, "Grow up! This is the real world, you know. You are talking about a dream world."

In the unfolding of the public ministry of Jesus as it is seen by the Evangelists and as it is looked at retrospectively in the Acts of the Apostles, we see that Jesus is the one who acts as though God reigned and nobody else had any power. Seeing Jesus this way had a startling impact on people.

They knew he had this kind of hope, and they knew they did not. And so, in their way, they stayed with him, but after his resurrection they realized that in a way they had it too. There was a breakthrough. The early Christians for some time lived in the first fervor of that, and they organized a Church. But the structure of the Church was not its life; structures do not beget life. Life means that generation after generation has to come alive and has to seize life personally as well as communally—something that cannot be done for people. Redemption is not something that is simply done for people like us. It is the empowerment for us to live in the grace of God, to live differently. The Ignatian tradition is a powerful resource for helping all Christians to become fully alive, to reflect the glory of God in the world, and to participate in the redemption of the world.

A Spirituality for Today. It will be evident from all of these five characteristics that Ignatian spirituality is a precious heritage in our own times and is particularly suitable to the contemporary circumstances of lay life after the Second Vatican Council. More possibilities and opportunities have been opened for us than have existed at any time since the third or fourth century. Thus it is a time to be fully, intelligently, and heartily alive to the Christian vocation.

Rich and Poor Churches and the Compassion Principle

Jon Sobrino, S.J.

In the Gospel, wealth and poverty are counterposed and even mutually exclusive realities. The former leads to damnation and the latter to salvation. The true Christian, thus, must be characterized by poverty and be opposed to wealth.

In a world of massive suffering, the mission of Christians can and, in my opinion, must be described in a nutshell as the exercise of compassion.[1] Along these lines, to put it in a way that is more than a play on words, I wish to argue that a Church rich in worldly terms is poor in compassion and that a Church poor in worldly terms is rich in compassion.

If I were making this presentation in Spanish, I would be using the word "misericordia," which can mean both "mercy" and "compassion." In the present context, I feel the latter is more appropriate; there are times, however, when I will use the former (as in "works of mercy") in deference to common usage.

Wealth Principle and Poverty Principle. To open the discussion, let me begin with the analysis made by Ignatius in the meditation on the Two Standards in his *Spiritual Exercises*.[2] It is true that this meditation is directed to the individual struggling for self-perfection. But the meditation can also be very well applied to the Church and its mission (or to a university, for that matter). Above all, Ignatius insists in that meditation on something which interests me very much: the way in which wealth and poverty have the nature of a "principle."

In effect, using a three-step approach, Ignatius presents two paths open to the Christian: one is the path of evil, the other the path of Jesus. But both paths have their own origin—wealth or poverty—which by their very nature determine the entire course of the journey. Wealth leads to vain worldly glory, which leads to pride, which in turn leads to all vices. Poverty leads to disgrace and scorn, which lead to humility, which in turn leads to all the virtues—or, in other words, to being human. These two paths are finally presented in a formal manner as antithetical and antagonistic, in such a way that in order to make progress on one path one must go against the other.

Let us examine how these principles take shape in history and see how they can be applied to an analysis of a wealthy Church and a poor Church, from the standpoint of today's world, a world which for the most part is impoverished and suffering.

A Church Shaped by the Wealth Principle. The path of evil begins with wealth, which, from a Gospel point of view, is an absolute ipso facto negation of the way to follow Jesus. For the Church, therefore, this is clearly the wrong path. But to this evangelical assertion of principles I must insist on adding another principle which is no less important. In a world in which the majority are poor,[3] wealth by its very nature leads the Church to distance itself from, disassociate itself from, and lose understanding of the real world. A wealthy Church is, above all, a Church which has not become incarnated in an overwhelmingly poor world; it thus becomes irrelevant and, in this sense, unreal. Not only is it not a Christian Church, since it does not follow the poor and humble Jesus, but it is also not a human Church. The former makes it ineligible as a sacrament of Christ, and the latter makes it ineligible as a sacrament of humanity. Both sacraments are demanded of the Church in the first section of *Lumen Gentium*. A wealthy Church has neither Christian identity nor Christian relevance.

Furthermore, when that Church establishes itself in the sinful, minority world of wealth, it ceases being "of this world" (incarnate), becoming instead "worldly," established in the "honors" of the world of which Ignatius speaks. From there it is led into "pride," by becoming an oppressive Church, and from there into "all vices" by participating in the greatest wrongs of humanity today, which can be expressed by the two following phenomena.

First, the world of wealth is overwhelmed with idols and is necessarily founded upon them. When situated amid wealth, one is inexorably drawn into relationships with its idols, and the greatest temptation is to worship them. All of what I say is perfectly compatible with nonreligious or nonbelieving ideologies, but also with religious ideologies. These idols require sacrificial offerings in order to subsist, and worshiping them thus means furnishing them with sacrificial offerings. In doing so the greatest evil of the entire wealth principle is revealed: It leads to killing. And let us recall that, in the gospel according to John, evil is "an assassin."

Second, idols seek to conceal themselves. They cover themselves up and even distort their essence ("the hour is coming when whoever kills you will think he is offering service to God"). And since the greater the outcry the greater the concealment, the idols of their very nature generate and require lies. And once again, let us recall that, in the gospel according to John, evil is also the "liar."

Such is the world of wealth. It is a world in which the Fifth and Seventh Commandments—the commandments which defend life and the basic means of life—are massively and structurally violated. This is a world in which the Eighth Commandment is also massively and structurally violated in the concealment of the fundamental violation of the will of God. By this I mean that the Eighth Commandment, which touches upon the world of lies and structural concealment, is an issue practically overlooked by the social doctrine of the Church. This is even more surprising given that the Church is an institution substantially based on words, and the word is the vehicle of both truth and lies, of unmasking and of concealment.

To be situated in the world of wealth is in and of itself de-Christianizing and dehumanizing. But, for the Church, the worst part of its active involvement in that world is that it is introduced—consciously or not, willingly or not—into a sinful dynamic which leads it—actively or passively, by action or by omission—to establish itself and participate in the greatest worldly sin, at least in a structural manner.

A Church Shaped by the Poverty Principle. The path of Jesus begins with poverty, and from a Gospel point of view, that is where a

Christian Church should begin. But poverty should be the place of the Church from an historical point of view as well.

In an impoverished world, the Church should be located amid poverty simply in order to be real. The importance of the Church becoming a real phenomenon in an overwhelmingly poor world can be graphically seen in the prophetic words of Archbishop Romero: "Brothers, I am glad that the Church is persecuted. That shows that it has become incarnated in poverty." And in these even more chilling words: "It would be very sad if, in a country where Salvadorans are so horribly assassinated, no priests were to be assassinated." The words are hair-raising, but what matters is the lesson: It is fundamental for the Church to be immersed in the true reality of the world, and this is not a matter of intentions, nor of pure formality—wherever one may be—but rather of being truly immersed in the most exigent moment of reality. As long as the reality of this world is poverty, the Church can have no other place.

In an impoverished world, the Church should be located amid poverty simply in order to be real.

The internal dynamics of this poverty is something that Ignatius calls "disgrace and scorn." In this way poverty resolves the Church's great problem of being properly situated within the world (of the poor), without being sinfully of the world (of the rich), being of this world without being worldly. Reality shows this without a shadow of a doubt: a Church which lives and acts in the world of the poor and for the benefit of the poor is a defamed, threatened, persecuted, and martyred Church. In this way, poverty leads the Church to resemble Jesus and to provide the greatest goods—antithetical to the greatest evils of wealth—provided by Jesus and demanded by the reality of the world.

Contrary to idolatry, its incarnation in the poor leads the Church to defend the victims, denounce the idols, and announce the God of life. The Church, as if by its very nature, thus becomes the bearer of *euaggelion*, of good news and of good reality for the poor of this world. If evil is an assassin and takes away life, the poor Church gives life, and life in abundance.

Contrary to lies and concealment, poverty leads to truth and light. The Church, as if by its very nature, thus becomes a light in the darkness and truth amid the lies. If evil is a liar, the poor Church is the bearer of truth and light.

The Church's Need to Choose and the Difficulty of Choosing. Wealth and poverty are thus realties which are essential for describing a false or a true Church; but to consider poverty and wealth as "principles" of a process—"in a three-step manner," as Ignatius insists—also helps to verify if in fact there are rich churches and poor churches. If the Church is showered with honors and if it establishes itself among them with pleasure, then that Church has let itself be governed by the wealth principle, whether or not it admits it; and the worst of it is that such a Church will tend to participate in the sins of the world in which it has established itself. And inversely, if the Church is showered with the "disgraces" of the sinful world and it establishes itself within the oppressed world, then that Church has let itself be governed by the poverty principle; and, most importantly, that Church will tend to wipe sin from the face of the earth.

The conclusion to be drawn from all this is clear: The Church must be governed by the poverty principle, it must be a Church of the poor. But in being so fundamentally governed, there are two issues that must be clarified. The first is obvious: It is not easy to be governed by the poverty principle, not only because of its intrinsic difficulty, but also because the poverty principle works actively against it. To be situated in poverty is to be there as opposed to wealth.[4] And so the question arises as to what is strong enough to situate the Church in poverty and keep it there. The second issue is that, no matter how essential the poverty principle, it must be considered not simply as the structuring principle within the Church, but also as being at the service of its mission.

In my opinion, what historically facilitates the solution to both problems is the exercise of compassion. The Church must be situated in poverty because that facilitates the exercise of compassion, and this exercise of compassion is what in turn effectively keeps the Church identified with poverty and impoverishes it. There are undoubtedly other motives which drive the Church to situate itself in poverty, above all the example of Jesus; but we believe that the materiality of poverty is that which—existentially—best induces compassion, and the exercise of compassion is that which—once again existentially—best keeps the Church in poverty. Stated in simpler terms, a poor Church is, by its very nature, more compassionate, and a compassionate Church is, by its very nature, poorer. So let us examine the concept of a Church of compassion, but first of all let me explain what I understand by the compassion principle which must govern the Church.

THE COMPASSION PRINCIPLE. The term "compassion"[5] must be fully understood, since the word can have both true and good connotations as well as deficient and even dangerous connotations: feelings of compassion (with the danger that it may not go hand-in-hand with concrete practices), works of mercy (with the danger of not analyzing the causes of the suffering it seeks to address), meeting individual needs (with the danger of abandoning any attempt at transforming structures), welcoming attitudes (with the danger of paternalism). In order to avoid the limitations of the concept of "compassion" and the misunderstandings to which it lends itself, let us not simply speak of compassion, but rather of the "compassion principle," just as Ernst Bloch does not simply speak of hope, as if it were just one of many categorical realities, but rather of the "hope principle."

In the Beginning there Was Compassion. It is well known that in the beginning of the saving process there is a loving act on the part of God. "I have seen the affliction of my people who are in Egypt, and have heard their cry because of their taskmasters, I know their sufferings, and I have come down to deliver them" (Ex 3:7-8). The term used to describe this act on the part of God has a somewhat secondary importance, although the most adequate word would be "liberation." What I would like to highlight here, however, is the structure of the liberating movement: God hears the lamentations of a suffering people and, for that reason alone, decides to undertake a liberating action.[6]

We will use the word *compassion* to characterize this type of structured act of love. It must be said that (a) it is an action, actually more like a reaction to the internalization of the suffering of others, which has penetrated to the very core and heart (the suffering of an entire people, in this case, unjustly inflicted and affecting the basic levels of existence) and (b) the action is motivated by that suffering alone.

Internalizing the suffering of others is the beginning of the compassion reaction, but this in turn becomes the principle which shapes all God's actions: (a) not only is it seen in the beginning, but it also remains a fundamental constant throughout the entire Old Testament (God's partiality for victims just for being victims, God's active defense of them, and God's liberating designs for them); (b) taking that as a starting point, both the way in which the demand for justice takes shape in history and the denunciation of those who inflict unjust suffering take on their own logic; (c) through that action—not only because of it—and through successive acts of compassion God himself is revealed; and (d) the fundamental demand placed upon the human being and, in particular, on God's people is that they reenact God's compassion toward others, something which brings them closer to God.

> When Jesus wishes to give an example of the perfect human being, he tells the parable of the Good Samaritan.

To paraphrase the gospel, we could say that, if in the absolute divine beginning "was the Word" (Jn 1:1), and through this arose creation (Gen 1:1), in the absolute salvation-historical beginning "there was compassion" and this remains a constant in the saving process of God.

Compassion According to Jesus. This original compassion on the part of God is what takes shape in history through the practice and message of Jesus. The *misereor super turbas* is not only a regional attitude of Jesus, but rather the attitude which shapes his life and his mission, and which seals his fate. This attitude also shapes his vision of God and of the human being.

When Jesus wishes to give an example of the perfect human being, he tells the parable of the Good Samaritan. This is a solemn moment in the Gospel which goes farther than the curiosity of finding out which commandment carries the most weight. The parable seeks to tell us, in a word, what human beings are. Thus, the perfect human being is the one who saw a beaten man on the roadside, reacted, and aided him in every way he could. The parable does not tell us what the Good Samaritan was thinking or with what ultimate goal he acted. The only thing it says is that he did what he did because he "had compassion."

The perfect human being, then, is the one who internalizes the suffering of others—in the case of the parable, suffering that was unjustly inflicted—in such a way that the internalized suffering becomes a part of him or her and is transformed into the internal, original, and final principle which governs his or her behavior. Compassion—as a reaction—turns into the fundamental action characterizing the perfect human. This compassion, then, is not just one among many human realities, but rather the one that directly defines the human being. On the one hand, compassion is an insufficient term to define fully the human being, since he or she is also a being of knowledge, hope, and celebration; but, on the other hand, compassion is absolutely necessary. For Jesus, to be a human being is to react with compassion, and not to do so is to corrupt the human essence to the core, as occurred with the priest and the Levite who avoided the beaten man.

That compassion is also the reality with which the Gospel defines Jesus, who often heals the sick after hearing the plea to "have compassion" and acts because he feels compassion for the people. And that compassion is also used to describe God in another one of the key parables: the Father goes forth to meet his prodigal son, and when he sees him remorseful and bewildered, he "has compassion," reacts, embraces him, and organizes a feast.

If compassion can be used to describe human beings, Christ, and God, we are undoubtedly looking at something truly fundamental. Compassion is love, one could say in the context of the whole Christian tradition; but one must add that it is a specific form of love: love in practice which arises when one is confronted with the unjustly inflicted suffering of others[7] and acts to eliminate it for no other motive than the very existence of that suffering and without being able to offer any excuse for not doing so.

Elevating this compassion to a principle could seem like a minimal gesture, but without it, according to Jesus, there is no humanity or divinity and, as with all minimal gestures, it is truly a maximal one. What is important is that this minimal-maximal is the origin and the end: nothing exists before compassion to motivate it, and nothing exists beyond it which could renounce or relativize it.

In simple terms, this can be noted in the fact that Jesus presents the Samaritan as a polished example of someone who fulfills the commandment to love one's neighbor, but in the telling of the parable there is no indication whatsoever that the Samaritan assisted the beaten man along the road *in order to fulfill a commandment*, no matter how exalted, but rather because he simply "had compassion."

It is said that Jesus healed the sick, and at times he is depicted as annoyed because the healed do not thank him; but there is no indication whatsoever that he healed in order to be thanked (or in order to call attention in this way to his specialness or his divine powers), but rather because he "had compassion."

It is said that the heavenly Father welcomed his prodigal son, but there is no indication that this was a subtle tactic to obtain what he truly wanted—that his son confess his sins and thus put his life in order—but rather that he acted simply because he "had compassion."

Compassion, thus, is the origin and the end. It is not simply the categorical exercise of the so-called "works of mercy," although it could and should be expressed through these acts as well. It is something much more radical. It is a fundamental attitude that arises when one is faced with the suffering of others, when one reacts in order to eliminate it for the sole reason that such suffering exists, and with the conviction that in the reaction to the suffering of others that ought-not-to-exist, one's own existence is at stake with no other way out.

The parable shows that historical reality is rife with examples of a lack of compassion—as seen in the priest and the Levite. This is shocking to Jesus in and of itself; but the evangelists also show that, for Jesus, historical reality is shaped by an active anticompassion which wounds and kills human beings, and which also threatens and kills those who are governed by the compassion principle.

It is because he is compassionate—not because he is "liberal"—that Jesus decides to heal a man's withered hand even though it is the Sabbath. The argument he uses is obvious and simple: "Is it lawful on the Sabbath to do good or to do harm, to save life or to kill?" (Mk 3:4). His adversaries, however, are naturally described in terms which are antithetical to Jesus—"their hardness of heart" (3:5); they not only remain unconvinced, but also conspire against Jesus. Thus the story ends in a chilling fashion: "The Pharisees went out, and immediately held counsel with the Herodians against him, how to destroy him" (3:6).

Although the language of this passage from the Bible may be anachronistic, what is important is that it demonstrates the existence of compassion and anticompassion. As long as the former is reduced to feelings or pure works of mercy, the latter tolerates it; but when compassion is elevated to a principle and subordinates the Sabbath to the elimination of suffering, anticompassion reacts, because such behavior upsets the values of an oppressive world. As tragic as it may seem, Jesus died on the cross for having exercised compassion in an enduring fashion, until the end. Compassion, thus, is compassion which comes to be in spite of and opposed to anticompassion.

Yet in the face of this Jesus proclaims: "Blessed are the compassionate." The reason given by Jesus in the gospel according to Matthew seems to run along the lines of an eventual reward: "They shall obtain mercy." But the most fundamental reason is inherent. Whoever lives according to the compassion principle puts into practice the deepest essence of the human being: becoming closer to Jesus—the *homo verus* of the dogma—and to the heavenly Father. We might say, then, that this is what the theory of happiness offered by Jesus is all about: "Happy, blessed, are those who exercise compassion, the pure in heart, the peacemakers, those who hunger and thirst for righteousness, those who are persecuted for righteousness' sake, the poor. . . ." These are scandalous but enlightening words. Jesus wants all human beings to be happy, and the symbol of that happiness is to be together, the shared table. But as long as the great brotherly table of the kingdom of God does not appear in history, compassion must be exercised, and that, says Jesus, produces joy, happiness, delight.

The Compassion Principle. These brief reflections on compassion may help to clarify what I understand by the compassion principle. Compassion is not the only quality Jesus exercises, but it is what originally motivates him and shapes his entire life, mission, and destiny. The term "compassion" appears at times in the stories told in the Gospel, and sometimes it does not. But with or without that term, it is always behind Jesus' behavior when faced with the suffering of the great masses of people, the poor, the weak, those shorn of dignity, those who move him to the bottom of his heart. And this deeply moved heart is what shapes all that Jesus is: his knowledge, his hope, his actions, and his celebrations.

His hope, thus, is the same hope of the poor who have no hope and to whom he announces the kingdom of heaven. His practice is to benefit the small and oppressed (miracles of healing, exorcism of demons, embracing the sinners) and is against their oppressors (denouncing and unmasking them). His "social theory" is guided by the principle that massive and unjust suffering must be eliminated. His happiness is personal joy when the downtrodden understand, and his celebration is to sit at table with the marginalized. His vision of God is of a God who defends the downtrodden and is compassionate with the poor; and his fidelity to God is the other side of the coin of his decision to keep taking risks and suffer attacks brought on by his exercise of compassion. In the prayer by antonomasia, the Our Father, Jesus invites the helpless and destitute to call God their Father.

There is not enough space to go on much further on this topic. I only make note of it in order to provide a better understanding of what I mean by the "compassion principle." Compassion is present in the origins of what is divine and human. And human beings must be governed by that principle. Compassion informs all dimensions of one's human being: knowledge, hope, celebration, and of course practice. Each one has its own autonomy, but can and must be shaped and guided by one or another fundamental principle. That principle dominates all others. And so that this will not be seen as pure speculative recreation, it appears in the decisive passage of Matthew 25: whoever exercises compassion—whatever other dimensions of one's human reality are also exercised—has "gone into eternal life," has eternally become the perfect human being. The judge and the tribunals have compassion, and only compassion, as their guiding principle. It must be added that the criterion used by the judge is not arbitrary: God himself has demonstrated how one reacts with compassion to the lamentations of the oppressed, and thus the life of human beings is decided once they are faced with an answer to these lamentations.

THE "POOR" CHURCH AS A CHURCH "RICH IN COMPASSION." This compassion principle is what must be active in the Church of Jesus, and the pathos of compassion is what must inform and shape it. This means that the Church, inasmuch as it is a Church, must also reread the parable of the Good Samaritan with the same expectations, with the same fear and trembling with which Jesus' listeners heard it: What is fundamental, what is at stake? The Church must be and do many other things, but if the Church is not overflowing—insofar as it is Christian and human—with the compassion set forth in the parable, all other things will be irrelevant, and could even be dangerous if they try to pass for such a fundamental principle. Furthermore, this compassion, better than anything else, is what existentially situates the Church in the poverty of which we spoke earlier. If it is governed by the compassion principle, it will trace the steps called for by the poverty principle which, in the words of Ignatius, lead "to all virtues" and, in systematic language, lead to the true Church. We are aware that one cannot seek to establish a perfect parallel between the analysis we have offered of the compassion principle and Ignatius's analysis of the poverty principle. But all things considered, I believe that there is a close relationship between the two, and that both—poverty and compassion—reinforce each other.

Compassion Situates the Church in "Poverty" and Against "Wealth." The fundamental problem for the Church is to incarnate itself properly, to be in the right place. Formally speaking, that place is the world, a reality which is logically outside it; materially speaking, within the world is the reality of poverty. The exercise of compassion is what—by definition—draws the Church outside itself and takes it, not to any world (the world of culture, arts and science, for example, no matter how important these might be), but rather into the more primordial world of poverty, the world of those who are left beaten on the roadside—whether or not this world coincides physically and geographically with the intra-Church world. The world of poverty is the world of others' suffering, especially all the massive, cruel, and unjust suffering, where the lamentations of humanity are heard: "Were you there when they crucified my Lord?" as in the song of the oppressed African Americans of the United States, a phrase which contains more meaning than many pages of ecclesiology.

The place of the Church is, then, in poverty; and compassion is what effectively and existentially leads it to situate itself among poverty. If the crucified of this world are incapable of moving the hearts of the Church, drawing it out of itself and placing it at the base of their crosses, then who knows what else could be strong enough to get the Church to advance to the "first step" of poverty? The issue of what a poor Church really is could be discussed from here to eternity, and the casuistry used to determine the answer could lead to a dead end. But if the Church exercises compassion, at least one thing is clear: The Church is drawn out of itself and, at the same time, sets off on the road which leads to its rightful place—the world of poverty.

I would like to illustrate how crucial this is by using an important present-day example. It is quite common knowledge that it is not at all easy for the so-called institutional Church to step out of itself, much less to step into the world of poverty, but neither is it easy for the so-called progressive Church, nor for the purely progressive elements within it. It is certainly urgent, just, and necessary to demand human rights and freedom from within the Church—as the progressives do—especially for ethical reasons, because these are signs of brotherhood and sisterhood (and therefore signs of the kingdom of God) and because otherwise the Church has no credibility in today's world. But let us not forget that in this we are—logically—still inside the Church. As a logical priority, one must ask oneself how the rights to life and liberty are faring in the world. This latter emphasis is governed by the compassion principle, and Christianizes the first, but not necessarily vice versa. "Compassionate" Christianity may be progressive—as in Latin America—but progressive is sometimes not compassionate.

> *When the Church is drawn out of itself and sets off down the path along which the wounded are found, and remains on that path, then it is a different Church.*

I hope that what I have tried to show by this example has been well understood. The humanization of the Church from the inside out is an urgent task, but for the Church to think from the outside, from "the path" along which the wounded are found, is a primordial task. It is urgent for Christians, priests and theologians, for example, to demand their legitimate freedom within the Church, now restricted; but demanding freedom for millions of human beings who do not enjoy enough freedom to survive in the face of poverty or to live in the face of repression (or even to ask for a simple investigation of the crimes perpetrated against them) is even more urgent.

What I wish to illustrate with this example is how difficult is the task faced by the Church—including the progressive Church—in order to become incarnated in poverty; but I also wish to show the beginning of the solution: the exercise of compassion. When the Church is drawn out of itself, sets off down the path along which the wounded are found, and remains on that path—moved to compassion—then it is a different Church, at once a Church of compassion and a Church of poverty.

Compassion Leads the Church to Suffer "Disgrace and Scorn" as Opposed to "Vain Worldly Glory." In this world, "works of mercy" are applauded or tolerated, but a Church shaped by the compassion principle, which leads it to denounce the highway robbers who produce victims, to unmask the lies used to cover up oppression, and to encourage the victims to liberate themselves from oppression, is not tolerated. In other words, the highway robbers of the anticompassionate world tolerate the bandaging of wounds, but do not tolerate truly healing the wounded nor efforts to keep the wounded from once again falling into their hands.

When this happens, the Church, like any other institution, is defamed and persecuted—today's "disgrace and scorn"—which in turn proves that the Church has allowed itself to be governed by the compassion principle and is truly situated in poverty. And the absence of these threats, attacks, and persecution in turn proves that the Church has not allowed itself to be governed by the compassion principle and is instead situated in wealth.

The enduring exercise of compassion, defending the victims from the highway robbers, and not only helping them, leads one to be called "Samaritan." Today that name sounds very nice, precisely because that is what Jesus called the compassionate man, but let us recall that at the time it sounded very bad, and Jesus used it precisely for that reason, in order to emphasize the supremacy of compassion over religious concepts and in order to attack those religious persons who do not exercise compassion.

This continues to occur. Those who exercise the type of compassion not tolerated by the highway robbers are called all kinds of names today. In Latin America they are called subversives, Communists, liberationists, atheists. Lately, following the events in Eastern Europe, the names they are called can be less harsh: naive, anachronistic, outdated, and the like.

If anything is clear in today's world, it is the fact that the exercise of compassion leads to a loss of prestige and that "disgrace and scorn" are assured. A "good" Church is still (pejoratively) called "Samaritan." But that is not all. When the Church exercises enduring compassion—all the way to the final consequences—and denounces the highway robbers, it is disturbing the idols, "the forgotten gods" as J. L. Sicre correctly calls them—which does not mean that these gods have already been left behind; they are quite present and active, although carefully concealed. And so they react, kill, and submit the Church to the greatest possible disgraces and to the greatest form of impoverishment, which is death.

Compassion Leads to "Humility" as Opposed to "Pride." To persist in exercising compassion in the face of attack is no easy thing, but if this happens, the Church ascends to the step which Ignatius calls "humility" and which we might call the freedom within oneself to love and selflessly defend the victims, the freedom to exercise compassion until the final consequences. Archbishop Romero was a clear example of this. His actions involved him in painful personal and intra-Church conflicts and even put his life at risk. But they involved risking something even more difficult and seldom risked: the institution. And so, as he persisted in exercising compassion, he saw the Church's platforms destroyed: the radio and printing presses of the archdiocese, the high schools, and the universities. He saw how the institutional Church was decimated by arrests, deportations, and killings of the most important symbols of the institution: priests, religious women, catechists, delegates of the Word.

The Church was humiliated and distanced itself from "pride," from all power based upon worldly wealth and honor. But that humiliation also led it to freedom within, to truth, to grace: to "humility," as Ignatius said. In the wake of attacks and destruction of the Church, Archbishop Romero told his anguished listeners: "When they destroy our radio and kill our priests, know that they have not harmed us." And faced with the possibility of his own death, he said: "I have often been threatened with death. I must tell you that, as a Christian, I do not believe in death but instead in resurrection. If they kill me, I will be resurrected in the Salvadoran people. I say this to you without boasting, but rather with the deepest humility."

Such an attitude demonstrates that the exercise of compassion and the disgrace brought on by that exercise have had a purifying effect; they have led the Church to "humility" and have definitively distanced it from "pride." And from that point on, the Church is led to "all virtues" and away from "all vices."

Compassion Leads the Church to "All Virtues." Ignatius insists that proceeding through all three steps leads "to all other virtues." Proceeding from one to the next is not a mechanical process, and for that reason he uses the word "lead"; but it is also true that the intrinsic dynamic of each step is that it provides access to the next. If we apply this to the concept of compassion, a Church which allows itself to be truly governed by compassion ends up being a true Church, or at least a truer Church of Jesus than others.

An enduringly compassionate Church, one which has stayed on the path until the final consequences, is enlightened in such a way that it has a better view of what it must be and do. And, above all, it

The Compassion Principle

acquires the conviction that its fundamental guiding principle is truly compassion, that the principle with which it began is the one it must maintain always.

The Church also gains a clearer view of the content of its fundamental task, "how to tell the poor of this world that God loves them" (G. Gutiérrez); and of the need to provide a historical shape to that loving word of God, to give compassion a historical form and classify it in a hierarchical manner.

Everywhere one looks, one sees many types of physical and spiritual wounds. The severity and depth of these wounds vary greatly, and compassion must react in such a way as to heal them all. At the same time, the Church must not fall into a hasty generalization of wounds as if all were expressions of the same laments, nor should it invoke this generalization in order to justify its behavior by saying that it has always carried out works of mercy—though this is quite true. All human suffering deserves absolute respect and demands a response, but this does not mean that one must not somehow classify the wounds of today's world in a hierarchical manner.

> *All human suffering deserves absolute respect and demands a response.*

In each local Church there are undoubtedly specific physical and spiritual wounds, and all must be healed and bandaged. But since the Church is One and Catholic, one must first examine the health of that wounded person known as the world as a whole. Quantitatively, the greatest suffering on this planet of five billion human beings is the poverty which leads to death and the indignity that goes hand in hand with poverty, and this continues to be the greatest wound of all. And that great wound appears much more radically in the third world than in the first. Although this fact is known theoretically, it must be repeated: Just by having been born in El Salvador or Haiti or Bangladesh or Chad—as Ignacio Ellacuría said—one has much less life and very much less dignity than one who is born in the United States, Germany, or Spain. This is today's fundamental wound, and this means that what is wounded is God's very own creation.

This greatest wound of all is also the greatest wound for any Church, given the magnitude of the phenomenon in and of itself, and also given the responsibility for it which is shared by local institutions—governments, political parties, armies, trade unions, universities, and also churches. If a local church does not minister to that worldly wound, it cannot be said that it is governed by the compassion principle.[8]

Nothing of what we have said above detracts from the fact that local wounds (for example, the so-called fourth world inside the first, and other specific wounds of the first world such as the selfish individualism and linear positivism that deprive one of feelings and faith) must be ministered to as well. All these must be ministered to with compassion, but without relegating to the background that which is primordial, and even asking oneself if part of the root of such senselessness—this cultural malaise—does not perhaps stem, consciously or unconsciously, from one's shared responsibility for having produced a planet overwhelmingly wounded by poverty and indignity.

> *The fundamental mission of the Church is to put its faith at the service of the liberation of the oppressed.*

The above reflection is not obvious, although it may seem so. It is not usually shared, with full conviction, by many churches, and the fundamental reason for that, in my opinion, is that it is not really evident that the heart is pure enough to see the truth. To arrive at the truth—one of the "other virtues" mentioned by Ignatius—presupposes a correct subjective attitude, but, structurally speaking, it also presupposes a material existence which facilitates subjective honesty. What leads one to put into effect the possibilities of subjectivity which allow one to see the truth of this world is the material existence of poverty and the subsequent reaction of enduring compassion. For a Church which has reacted to the wounded found along the road, and which has consequently suffered the greatest defamation and "humiliation"—martyrdom—it is much easier to be enlightened about the true reality of humanity. Enduring compassion makes one "see" the truth, a truth not easily seen separately from the enduring exercise of such compassion.

What is already foretold in the Gospel becomes current reality: There is light in the suffering serf, knowledge in the crucified. But in order to gain light and knowledge, one must be there alongside the serf and the crucified. And if, above and beyond just being there, one attempts to take them down off the cross, one's light shines even brighter, and one gains the fundamental and unshakable conviction that the greatest evil of this earth is injustice and oppression, which produce poverty and indignity and broken brotherhood, and that the fundamental mission of the Church is to put its faith at the service of the liberation of the oppressed, also with the conviction that the practice of liberation illuminates one's faith.

This light which comes from the exercise of compassion is only an example, although a fundamental one, of how a Church can achieve the "other virtues." As Ignacio Ellacuría said, the fact that liberation theology has struck a chord in the people is not fundamentally due to the fact that its theologians are more knowledgeable than others, but rather that it finds itself in the right place. For a Church to allow itself to be governed by the compassion principle is to allow itself to be led to the right place; once there, it shines brighter.

What I have said up to this point is just an example, although an important one, of "the other virtues" to which the exercise of enduring compassion leads the Church. Let me add that, from the standpoint of compassion, its faith becomes a faith in the God of the wounded found along the road, in the God of the victims, in the God of life. Its liturgy celebrates the life of those without life, the resurrection of the crucified. Its theology is *intellectus misericordiae (justitiae, liberationis)*, and the theology of liberation is nothing but that. Its social doctrine and practice is an eagerness, in theory and in practice, to offer and travel effective roads to justice.[9] Its ecumenism comes to life and prospers—and history shows this—in the presence of crucified peoples who, like Christ, draw others around them.

It is necessary for the Church to react with compassion in order to achieve "all virtues," to be more truly a Church of Jesus. And I add that this is possible because it indeed happens, and for that reason these pages—whatever their destiny—are based upon the real-life study of a Church which has taken absolutely seriously the concept of reacting with compassion. What we would like to insist upon is the fact that this possibility became reality not as a product of intentional voluntarism, nor from sticking purely to textbooks—past or present, sacred or profane—but rather through the exercise of compassion.

Let me close with two brief reflections upon the fullness to which the exercise of compassion leads the Church. The first is that compassion is also a blessing, and a Church of compassion—if it is truly compassionate—is thus a Church which feels joy; and having joy, it can show it. And in this way—a fact often forgotten—the Church can communicate *in actu* that its news, in word and deed, is *euaggelion*, the good news that not only represents the truth, but also brings joy. A Church which does not spread joy is not the Church of the Gospel; it must not, of course, spread just any kind of joy, but rather the kind of joy that is provided and heralded in its founding charter, the Beatitudes, among which is found the joy of compassion.

The second reflection is that a Church of compassion of the kind described above is noticed in today's world. And it is noticed in a particular fashion: with credibility. The credibility of the Church depends on several factors, and in democratic and culturally developed worlds it must include the exercise of freedom within the Church and a rational presentation of the message which awards it respectability. But I believe that in all the world, which includes the nations of the first world, the greatest credibility is generated by enduring compassion, precisely because it is the element most lacking in the world today. A Church of compassion is at the very least credible, and if it is not enduring in its compassion, in vain will it seek credibility by other means. Among those who are fed up with the faith, among agnostics and unbelievers, that Church will at least make the name of God respectable, and God will not be cursed for what the Church does or fails to do. That Church will win acceptance and gratitude among the poor of this world. A Church of compassion is the one which is noticed in today's world, and is noticed in the way God intended. For that reason, compassion is the key indication that the true Church of Jesus exists.

All that has been said in this article is nothing more than a restatement of the well-known option for the poor which the Church must exercise in accordance with the declarations of the institutional Church itself. Thus what I have said is not new, although perhaps it contributes to an understanding of the radicality, primordiality, and finality of that option. In theory, all agree that the Church must today be a Church of the poor. What I have attempted to clarify is that there is an inherent relationship between poverty and compassion, and that existentially the best way for the Church to situate itself in the difficult world of poverty is to react with compassion. A poor Church is a Church which is inclined toward compassion. And a compassionate Church is a Church which is led into poverty.

NOTES

[1] In support of this position, it is enough to recall that the mission of Jesus was to announce and make real the kingdom of God for the poor, who were considered the victims of the powers of this world.

[2] *Spiritual Exercises,* nos. 136-198. In our opinion, the structure of the treatment of wealth and poverty, if taken in its proper historical context, continues to be quite applicable in today's world. I hope that this meditation, which touches upon the most critical problem in our world today, is kept in mind during the celebration of the Ignatian anniversaries.

[3] In the first world, especially following the events of Eastern Europe, there is a type of euphoria which leads one to ignore poverty in the third world. In Latin America, things are not only not improving, but are even getting worse. To illustrate this in just one simple figure: The U.N. Economic Commission on Latin America (CEPAL) said on October 4, 1990, that Latin America needs $90 billion in order for per capita income in 1995 to reach 1980 levels.

[4] Ignatius was very insightful in expressing the antithetical nature of the two principles: poverty vs. wealth, disgrace and scorn vs. worldly honor, humility vs. pride (no. 146).

[5] What I say in the following paragraphs about compassion has already been substantially discussed in an article in the October 1990 issue of the magazine *Sal Terrae,* "The Samaritan Church and the Compassion Principle."

[6] J. L. Segundo, in his book *Liberation Theology: Response to Cardinal Ratzinger* (Madrid, 1985), pp. 61ff, demonstrates in detail that the final aim of the Exodus is simply the liberation of a suffering people, contrary to the first Vatican instruction on liberation theology, according to which the final aim of the Exodus is the foundation of the people of God and the cult of the Covenant in the Sinai.

[7] Compassion must also turn its attention to "natural" suffering, but we believe that its ultimate essence is expressed in ministering to those who suffer as "victims," whether of natural or historical adversities; in the Gospel greater importance is generally accorded to the victims of history than to the victims of natural phenomena.

[8] Stated without bitterness and with simple fraternal feelings, it is surprising that throughout the last ten tumultuous years of history (and Church life) in El Salvador, virtually no Spanish bishop has visited this country and its Church, with the exception of the bishop in charge of missions and Alberto Iniesta, who came for Archbishop Romero's funeral and who was encouraged and funded by his parishioners in Vallecas.

[9] It is very clear to me that Ignacio Ellacuría allowed himself to be governed by the compassion principle in all his activities and particularly in his intellectual, theological, and philosophical activities as well as his political analysis. I mention this in order to underline the fact that compassion is much more than just pure feeling or pure compassionate activism. It is also the principle which shapes the exercise of the intellect.

The Greater Glory of God: Woman Fully Alive

Elizabeth A. Johnson, C.S.J.

W<small>E ARE GATHERED IN A SPIRIT OF CELEBRATION</small>, to mark the five hundredth anniversary of Ignatius Loyola's birth, and the four hundred fiftieth year since the founding of the Society of Jesus. To all the members of the Society I say "Happy anniversary!" and, in the words of an old Latin toast, "*ad multos annos.*" The guiding idea of this celebrative lecture series is Ignatian spirituality as a resource for living the faith today. I could think of no better element of Ignatian spirituality to reflect upon than the maxim *ad maiorem Dei gloriam*: to the greater glory of God. We might call it Ignatius's theme song, for it was an expression of his enthusiasm for Christ, to whom he was passionately attached.[1] Over the years this axiom has become so widely known that it now belongs to the whole Church.

As Ignatius used the phrase in his writings, each of its words has a very definite meaning.

Dei gloriam: the glory of God, has a double-sided sense. From God's side it signifies divine majesty, the radiance of divine greatness shining on the world. From the human side it connotes the response of giving praise to God by wholehearted apostolic service. The two meanings intertwine in the customary way Ignatius uses the axiom to speak about moments of decision. A person must then discern where the divine purpose can best be promoted through the use of our precious human energy.

Maiorem: greater. This is the vocabulary of the heart. It signifies great élan, more love, wholehearted passion for God's glory in the whole of life.

Ad: toward. This small preposition releases a great vision. The end is not yet attained. There is still more to do, for God's will is not yet done on earth as it is in heaven. The *ad* charges this motto with eschatological value, pressing it toward the future which is promised but unknown.

Ad maiorem Dei gloriam: the whole motto gives a dynamic orientation to life, enthusiastic for God.

I propose to reflect on how this motto may serve as a resource for spirituality amid today's complexities. In doing so I will risk a feminist interpretation of this influential maxim. By a feminist interpretation I mean one that endorses women's full and equal human dignity, and advocates ways to promote this human dignity in every dimension of society and church.[2] Such a perspective in theology and spirituality is aware of women the world over awakening to their own equal human dignity, to the ways women's humanity is suppressed in the church and society, and to imaginative vision and actions that would rebirth the world in a more just and loving way. What does *ad maiorem Dei gloriam* have to do with the lives of women and with women's flourishing?

We will explore this question in three points. First we lay the groundwork by examining the meaning of the glory of God in biblical and patristic tradition. Next we investigate how sexism dims that glory, promoting not the greater but the lesser glory of God. From this it will become clear, finally, how women's emancipation, so essential for building a human community of mutuality, promotes the glory of God, truly serving the life project of making choices in view of the *greater* glory of God.

THE GLORY OF GOD IN BIBLICAL AND PATRISTIC TEXTS. When Scripture speaks of glory in relation to creatures, the term usually refers to worldly splendor and magnificence. Not even Solomon in all his glory was arrayed more beautifully than the lilies of the field which, in Jesus' memorable example, neither toil nor spin (Mt 6:28-29). But when the Bible speaks of God's glory, then the word takes on a different meaning.[3] For God is the creator, redeemer, judge, and lover of the world, and this entails that divine glory freely ties itself to the world's well-being.

In the Hebrew Scriptures the word for glory is *kabod*, loosely translated as a weighty radiance or dark brightness. The *kabod YHWH* is divine power shining through the world's darkness, drawing near and passing by to enlighten, warm, and free from captivity. The Exodus narrative makes great play with this symbol, using it to speak about the presence of the God of the Israelites acting to free them from slavery. "Show me thy glory," Moses prays, and receives the answer that he will see it when God's goodness passes by (Ex 33:18-19). In the theophany at Sinai the weighty radiance of divine glory is depicted in turn as a cloud and a devouring fire (Ex 24:15-18); through the long trek back to the promised land the glory of the Lord accompanies the Israelites, tents among them, and guides them as a pillar of cloud by day and a pillar of fire by night, delivering them into safety at last (Ex 40:34-38).

> *Biblically the glory of God signifies God's power bent over brokenness and anguish, moving to heal, redeem, and set free.*

Centuries later the people are again in captivity, this time in Babylon. Uttering words of comfort, the prophet Isaiah proclaims that "the glory of the Lord will be revealed" (Is 40:5). When will this happen? When they are released from exile and allowed to return home. Then they will see a resplendent manifestation of God's power in a historical moment of liberation and homecoming, sign of that future day when evil will be overcome, the lion will lie down with the lamb, the reign of *shalom* will begin.

Biblically the glory of God does not point to God as a bigger and better Solomon, sitting on a throne in isolated splendor. Rather, it signifies God's power bent over brokenness and anguish, moving to heal, redeem, and set free. It is a synonym for God's presence and action in the midst of suffering people. As such it is a category of relation and help.

The Christian Scriptures use the Greek word *doxa* to speak about the weighty radiance of God's glory. With the coming of Jesus the Christ, divine power and care are concentrated in a new way. Now God's glory shines through the night of sin and death, not in the form of fire or cloud, but in the very human flesh of Emmanuel, God with us.

When he is born the angels sing, "Glory to God in the highest, and on earth peace. . . ." (Lk 2:14), proclaiming the Jewish insight that divine glory and human good in tandem are two different sides of the same coin. The ministry of Jesus makes strikingly manifest how God's glory operates: the blind see, the lame walk, the dead are raised up, the poor have the good news preached to them (Mt 11:5). In an antagonistic world this is not accomplished without cost. Jesus is crucified, but through the power of the Spirit he is raised into glory and lives a life in the glory of God that is shared with the women and men who follow him and form his body. This solidarity with Christ crucified and risen empowers the Christian vocation. Paul encouraged the Corinthians, "Whether you eat or drink, or whatever you do, do all to the glory of God" (1 Cor 10:31). Glory, then, is a category of participation in God's great redeeming love that draws near to share the brokenness of the world in order to heal and set free.

The biblical notion of God's glory consistently faces us toward the future and the eschatological fullness of the last day. Then God's glory will fill the universe. The whole city will be radiant with God's glory. We will not even need the sun, for God's glory will be our light. And what will God's glory be doing? After all the suffering, it will be wiping away every tear from our eyes, and there will be no more death or mourning or crying out (Rv 21:4). Humanity redeemed, in a new heaven and new earth: herein lies the glory of God.

In the second century the bishop and theologian Irenaeus crystallized the biblical notion of God's glory in an axiom almost as well known as Ignatius's. Carrying forward the tradition of Exodus and Easter, he consistently wrote that *Gloria Dei vivens homo*: the glory of God is *homo*—the human being, the whole human race including every individual person—fully alive. Because God is the creator, redeemer, and lover of human beings who are made in the divine image, God's own honor is at stake in human happiness. Wherever *homo* is violated or diminished or has life drained away, God's glory is dimmed and dishonored. Wherever *homo* is quickened to fuller and richer life, God's glory is enhanced. A community of justice and peace—which is a thriving among human beings—and God's glory increase in direct and not inverse proportion.

Given the destructive power of evil and the anguish of suffering, both the mystery of God's glory and human flourishing are terrifyingly at risk in history. Both are in mutual jeopardy. Sin and violence give to Irenaeus's well-loved axiom the character of hope against hope. But, as it stands, it sums up the entire witness of the Scriptures. The glory of God, by God's own choice, is at stake in human flourishing and in the well-being of the whole world.

Ignatius's axiom *ad maiorem Dei gloriam,* to the greater glory of God, is rightly interpreted as a resource for spirituality today when set within the biblical and patristic insight that *Gloria Dei vivens homo,* the glory of God lies in human flourishing. Such a view is implicit in the *Spiritual Exercises* and other Ignatian writings. Whatever we do should be aimed at glorifying God by resisting what destroys God's beloved creatures, *homo,* and fostering what heals, redeems, and liberates every dimension of the world which God so loves. Rooted in this mystery of God's graciousness, we turn to our neighbors in need, and through our apostolic service, directly or through structural change, promote their salvation.

S<small>EXISM</small>: T<small>OWARD THE</small> L<small>ESSER</small> G<small>LORY OF</small> G<small>OD</small>. A most basic question is being raised by women today: Are we, too, genuinely human? If the answer given is yes, if women, too, are really and fundamentally human, with a nature that is essentially human nature, intrinsically belonging to the human race, created in the image and likeness of God, God's beloved creature, then women are to be designated *homo,* as are men. Then the ancient maxim can be pressed to a critical, concrete focus and declare that *Gloria Dei vivens mulier:* the glory of God is woman, all women, every woman everywhere, fully alive.

Because God is the creator, redeemer, lover of women, who are made in the divine image, God's own honor is at stake in women's happiness. Wherever women are violated, diminished, have life drained away, God's glory is dimmed and put at historical risk. Where women are quickened to fuller and richer life, God's glory is enhanced. A human community of justice and peace—inclusive of women's flourishing—and God's glory increase in direct and not inverse proportion.

Sexism. Throughout history this concrete version of the ancient maxim has been honored more in the breach than in reality due to the pervasiveness of sexism, which both drafts of the U.S. bishops' pastoral letter on women's concerns rightly call a sin.[4] We dwell on this the better to ascertain the depths of the violation done to God's glory by the dishonor done to women.

Sexism, in Margaret Farley's generic description, is "belief that persons are superior or inferior to one another on the basis of their sex. It includes attitudes, value systems, and social patterns which express or support this belief."[5] Historically, sexism maintains that persons of the male sex are inherently superior to persons of the female sex by nature, that is, according to the laws of creation, and it acts in discriminatory ways to enforce this natural order.

Sexism is prejudice pure and simple. In a pattern that parallels racism, this prejudice classifies one group of human beings as deficient, prescribes certain subordinate roles for them, and denies them certain rights on the basis of physical and/or psychological characteristics alone. Just as racism assigns an inferior dignity to people on the basis of their skin color or ethnic heritage, so too sexism views women on the basis of biological sex as essentially less valuable than men, and labors mightily to keep them in their "proper" social "place." In both isms bodily characteristics are made to count for the whole essence of the human being, so that the fundamental dignity of the person is violated. Sexism, like racism, betrays the fundamental inability of a dominant group to deal with otherness, to acknowledge equal humanity and kinship with those who are different from oneself. Instead, it structures a world oriented to the benefit of men, the value of men, and the normativity of men.

Women experience the effects of sexism both socially and psychologically, in the Church as well as in society. As the feminist axiom "the personal is the political" insightfully acknowledges, the two cannot be divorced. The litany of examples is long and painful.

For most of history women have been denied political, economic, legal, and educational rights. In no country in the world are women's rights yet equal to those of men in practice. In situations where people suffer intolerably from poverty and racism, the dynamic of sexism burdens women with added and profound exploitation. They are the underclass who function as "slaves to the slaves," subordinated to men who themselves are already oppressed. Women, according to United Nations statistics, while forming more than one-half of the world's population, work two-thirds of the world's working hours, own one-tenth of the world's wealth and one-hundredth of the world's land, and form two-thirds of the world's illiterate people. Over three-fourths of starving people are women with their dependent children.[6] To make a dark picture even bleaker, women are bodily and sexually exploited, physically abused, raped, battered, and murdered. The indisputable fact is that men do this to women in a way that women do not do it to men. Sexism is rampant on a global scale.[7] Is this *ad maiorem Dei gloriam?*

In the Church the prejudice of sexism shows itself in analogous ways. For most of history women have been subordinated in theological theory and ecclesial practice at every turn. They have been consistently defined, until as recently as 1983, as mentally, morally, and physically inferior to men, as not created in the image of God in their own right. They have even been regarded as a degrading symbol of evil: woman as temptress (to men, of course). Women's sexuality has been derided as unclean; or, conversely, they have been depersonalized and put on a pedestal as a romantic, unsexed ideal. Women are excluded from centers of significant decision-making, law-making, and symbol-making, and prevented from exercising public leadership roles. They are excluded from full participation in the sacramental system; yet they are expected to be recipients of God's grace through that sacramental system administered exclusively by men. They are made invisible in generic, male-dominated language, and their femaleness is judged unsuitable for speech about God. They are expected to relate to a male Savior sent by a male God whose legitimate representatives can only be male, all of which relegates their persons as women to the periphery of the central story.

In a word, women occupy a marginal place in the official life of the Church: They are necessarily there but of restricted value.[8] Is this *ad maiorem Dei gloriam?*

The social structure of ecclesial sexism, known as patriarchy,

> *Women are excluded from full participation in the sacramental system; yet they are expected to be recipients of God's grace through that sacramental system administered exclusively by men.*

has profound psychological and spiritual effects. To give but one example: For women, speech about God couched exclusively in male images does not point to the equal participation of women and men in the divine ground. Male images allow men to participate fully in it, while women can do so only by abstracting themselves from their concrete, bodily identity as women. Thus is set up a largely unconscious dynamic which alienates women from their own goodness and power at the same time it reinforces dependency upon men and male authority. Carol Christ has analyzed this in particularly acute fashion. If God is spoken about solely in male terms, then woman

> may see herself as like God (created in the image of God) only by denying her own sexual identity and affirming God's transcendence of sexual identity. But she can never have the experience that is freely available to every man and boy in her culture, of having her full sexual identity affirmed as being in the image and likeness of God.... Her "mood" is one of trust in male power as salvific and distrust of female power in herself and other women as inferior and dangerous.[9]

Typical ecclesial language describing God in the exclusive and literal image of a patriarch functions as a tool of subtle conditioning which debilitates women's sense of dignity, power, and self-esteem. Is this *ad maiorem Dei gloriam?*

It is crucial to note that ecclesial prejudice against women does not occur by accident. It occurs with the conscious belief that this order of things is God's will, that God is glorified by men's superiority over women. A gruesome symbol of this idea appears during the era of the Inquisition in seventeenth-century Europe when thousands, perhaps hundreds of thousands of women were put on trial as witches in church courts and executed in the name of God. This is a very public though by now suppressed and rarely told chapter in the history of women's affliction. The poet Robin Morgan has composed a litany of remembrance of forgotten women:

> Margaret Jones, midwife, hanged 1648.
> Joan Peterson, veterinarian, hanged 1652.
> Isobel Insch Taylor, herbalist, burned 1618.
> Barbara Gobel, described by her jailers as "the fairest maid in Wurzburg," burned 1645.
> Frau Peller, raped by Inquisition torturers because her sister refused the judge Franz Buirman, 1631.
> Sybille Lutz, burned 1628, 11 years old.
> Emerzianne Pichler, tortured and burned together with her two children, 1679.

> Frau Dumler, boiled to death in hot oil while pregnant, 1630.
> Sister Maria Renata Sanger, subprioress of the Convent of UnterZell, accused of being a lesbian; [and here is where the ghastly symbol appears] the document certifying her torture is inscribed with the words, "AD MAJOREM DEI GLORIAM."[10]

Is it?

The litany is practically endless, and could be extended to include all the women throughout the generations who have been killed, beaten, raped, ruined, or demeaned by men's ignorance, hatred, and obsession with their own righteousness and rule. This is not to say that all men do this, for obviously some act in ways directly contrary to such violation. But it is to say that sexism shapes the public culture of church and society, and stacks the deck against women in every round.

The prejudice against the genuine humanity of women, so harmful to women's flourishing, is a sign of the broken mutuality between the sexes, a fractured human community that overshadows the glory of God.

Sexism, finally, does not stand alone but interlocks with racism, economic classism, militarism and cultural imperialism, and with the destruction of the life-systems of the earth.[11] The fundamental sin is exploitation, whether it is expressed in the domination of male over female, white over black, rich over poor, strong over weak, armed military over unarmed civilians, human beings over nature. These abusive patterns interlock because they rest on the same base: a structure where an elite insists on its superiority and claims the right to exercise dominative power over all others considered subordinate, for its own benefit.

Sexism is foundational to these abusive patterns: Does there exist anywhere on this planet a military dictator who denies economic justice to the poor and yet believes in the equality of women? Historically the subjugation of women may in fact be the original oppressor/oppressed relation, and thus the working paradigm for all others. In her study of the creation of patriarchy, Gerda Lerner argues for this view, tracing the origin of domination back to the situation when, after victory in war, men killed the conquered men but forcibly took women of conquered groups into their own harems or households. They were thereby learning skills and techniques of domination which could eventually be applied to conquered men as well.[12]

If not historically, then at least qualitatively, in classical Western culture the priority of male over female served as the paradigm of oppressive relationships. The self-image of ruling-class men in the golden age of Greece allowed them to claim that they alone intrinsically possessed the true human qualities of spirit, initiative, reason, capacity for autonomy and higher virtue. Women are projected as the "other," the repository for qualities such as bodiliness and feeling that men cannot integrate into their self-image and therefore the antithesis against which they define themselves. This repressive view of the alien female then serves as the basic model for projecting views of inferiority onto other subjugated groups, lower classes, conquered races, nonhuman creatures.[13]

The interlocking of oppressions deepens the feminist theological agenda. Addressing the question of the subordination of women brings into view the entire structure of what has commonly been taken to be "reality." What is being looked for is not simply the solution to one problem, but an entire shift of worldview away from patterns of dominance toward mutually enhancing relationships. One feminist song states, "the rising of the women is the rising of the race" precisely because women with their network of relationships are at the lowest ebb, marginalized, silenced, made invisible, even as they sustain every society. The incoming tide lifts all the boats in the harbor.

Scotosis. It is not uncommon for people whose certitudes and securities may be threatened by the question of women's flourishing to relegate it to the periphery of importance, calling it merely a "woman's question." Bernard Lonergan has a pointed name for such a hardening of the mind against unwanted wisdom. He calls this rigidity a "scotosis," and the resulting blind spot a "scotoma."[14] Scotosis results when the mind's intellectual censorship function, which usually operates in a good and constructive manner to select elements to give us insight, goes awry. In aberrant fashion this censorship function works to repress new questions in order to prevent the emergence of unwanted insight. This happens not only to an individual in isolation. Social groups are implicitly defined by the patterns of relationship that make up a given social order. Group interest limits intelligence insofar as a group is prone to have a blind spot for insight that would reveal its well-being to be excessive or to be founded on distorted assumptions. The tendency of such group bias is to exclude some fruitful ideas and to mutilate others by compromise.

Relegating the theological question of women's flourishing to the periphery of serious consideration is an instance of this phenomenon. It is the refusal of insight as a function of group bias. Regrettably this scotosis is widely observable in the Church today.

But feminism and the question it raises about the genuine human dignity of women cannot be so easily dismissed. It is a powerful worldwide phenomenon which deeply affects all aspects of social reality. Vatican II spoke eloquently about tradition as a living thing that can grow:

> For there is a growth in the understanding of the realities and the words which have been handed down. This happens through the contemplation and study made by believers who treasure these things in their hearts (Lk 2:19, 51), through the intimate understanding of spiritual things they experience....[15]

What the council did not envision but what is clearly happening today is that this growth in understanding is operative among believers who are women. Women believers are newly contemplating and studying things they have treasured and, through the intimate understanding of things they experience, are causing growth in the understanding of what has been handed down. In faith and struggle women are growing the Church into a new moment of the living tradition. As Anne Carr has so eloquently put it, the women's movement comes as a transforming grace for the whole Church—although, terrifyingly, grace may always be refused.[16]

WOMEN'S FLOURISHING: TOWARD THE GREATER GLORY OF GOD. Women worldwide today are struggling against sexism and its debilitating effects. In theological terms this is a struggle to take seriously their own female humanity as *imago Dei*, to make their God-given dignity historically tangible, and thereby to secure a foothold for the glory of God in history. This has vital religious significance. For in thus hearing and naming themselves in speech and engaging in transformative action, women are simultaneously involved in a new experience of God, which is of value for the whole Church.

Experience of Self. Women experience a breakthrough of power as they reject the sexism of tradition and risk new interpretations which affirm their own worth. This is a complex process that basically has the character of conversion.

The process begins with an experience of contradiction

between the suffering caused by sexism and the *humanum* of women, between the crushing on the one hand and women's own dignity on the other. The contrast between the one and the other gives rise to a profound and irrevocable "No, this should not be!" The judgment arises: We are worth more than this. Indignation and anger generate the energy for creative resistance, and the search commences in both action and theory for a release of the tension by changing the situation. In a classic sense what transpires here is a contrast experience, giving rise through the violation of a good to a glimpse of its strong value in a new configuration.[17]

The ringing "no" to women's denigration is a stance grounded on an equally deep and lasting "yes" to the fundamental humanity of women. In the midst of the suffering, a positive view of women's beauty and power as active subjects of history also arises. While consistently subordinated in official practices, women have nevertheless in fact always been actively present. They have acted in creative ways to live their own lives and bring about the good of others in the light of the Gospel. Despite its ambiguity with regard to women, the Christian tradition has served and continues to serve as a strong source of life for many women, our mothers and grandmothers in the faith throughout the centuries. Women's historical goodness reprised in contemporary self-affirmation is interpreted as empowerment by the Spirit in the following of Christ.

The ringing "no" to women's denigration is a stance grounded on an equally deep and lasting "yes" to the fundamental humanity of women.

Given the negative assessment of women's humanity under sexism, women's self-affirmation of themselves as subjects, active subjects of history—and as *good* ones—has the character of a conversion process, that is, a turning away from trivializing and defaming one's own being and a turning toward oneself as worthwhile—in fact, as a gift.

As Experience of God. The idea of God has very deep roots in the human person's experience of self. It follows that adjustments in the experience of one of these realities will of necessity affect experience of the other. As Karl Rahner analyzes it: "The personal history of the experience of oneself is at the same time the personal history of the experience of God."[18] They are two aspects of one and the same history of experience. Each mutually conditions the other.

Consequently, when a person claims the self in new freedom, or experiences hatred of self, or finds a new way of loving others and thus oneself, or affirms trustful acceptance of self, then the changing history of this self-relation also entails living through a changing history of the experience of God. Conversely, when a person destroys a false idol, or glimpses new truth about God, or transcends all particular categories in reverence toward mystery, these episodes in the history of one's experience of God are events directly belonging to the history of the self. To sum up, over a lifetime "the personal history of the experience of the self is in its total extent the history of the ultimate experience of God also."[19]

It is in this deeply personal-and-religious dimension of spirituality that women today are caught up in new experience of themselves which is also new experience of God. Women are naming themselves in goodness, power, responsibility, and freedom in mutual relatedness, and affirming themselves to be every bit as sinful as men but also every bit as graced.

"No" to the disparagement of sexism plus "yes" to one's own worth as God's beloved creature is a deeply religious event: the coming into being of suppressed selves. It releases a new experience of God who blesses women, who is beneficent toward the female and an ally of women's flourishing. Indeed, God can even be named in the image of the female.

Imago Dei, Imago Christi. When this experience is brought to speech it results in women's ownership of the doctrine of the image of God, image of Christ in all its fullness, precisely in their concrete reality as female.

Despite the exegesis of Augustine, Aquinas, and others of like patriarchal mind-set, the biblical creation story that portrays human beings created in the image of God originally intended the compliment for women and men equally (Gen 1:26-27). Male and female are in the divine image and likeness, each as themselves and both together. Their sexual difference is flagged in the story to highlight the fact that like other creatures human beings are gifted with fertility, the power to be fruitful and multiply. But there is no prizing of men over women in this Genesis story. *Homo* is in the image of God, and their reciprocal relationship forms a community of mutuality.[20]

Not incidentally, the *imago Dei* doctrine works both ways. If women are created in the image of God, without qualification, then their human reality offers suitable, even excellent, metaphor for speaking about divine mystery. In and through women's experience of their female selves as blessed comes language about holy mystery of God in female metaphors and symbols, gracefully, powerfully, necessarily.

In the Christian dispensation the baptismal tradition is radically egalitarian. Its ritual is inclusive, administered to women and men in the same way, unlike circumcision which restricted the rite of initiation to one part of the male anatomy. Its theology is likewise inclusive, for all who drink of the one Spirit in the waters of baptism form one body in Christ. "There is then no more Jew or Greek, slave or free, male or female, but all are one in Christ Jesus" (Gal 3:28). Broken by sinfulness though they be, the members of the community die and rise with Christ, are traced by the sign of the Spirit *en Christo*, and their own lives assume a Christic pattern.

This is clearly visible in the martyrdom tradition. Despite the restriction of Christhood to males by official Roman documents and others of like mind, the wider Church recognizes the identification between Christ and the female martyr. In the Acts of the Apostles, for example, we read:

> But Saul, still breathing threats and murder against the disciples of the Lord, went to the high priest and asked him for letters to the synagogues at Damascus, so that if he found any belonging to the Way, men or women, he might bring them bound to Jerusalem (Acts 9:1-5).

When the light from heaven flashes, when the mysterious voice asks "Why do you persecute me?", when Saul queries "Who are you, Lord?", the answer is profoundly instructive: "I am Jesus, whom you are persecuting." Both women and men disciples are here identified with Jesus without distinction. The same theological assessment is given to both. Saul's murderous intent and tormenting actions against women disciples are actions against Jesus Christ, without qualification.

Vatican II continues this long-standing tradition in its writing about the cloud of witnesses that surrounds us with the testimony of their lives. Martyrdom, writes the council, transforms a disciple into an image of Christ, *imago Christi*. Christ freely accepted death for the world's salvation; the martyr "perfects that image even to the shedding of blood."[21] In this text no distinctions are made on the basis of the martyrs' sex, nor should there be. The four North American churchwomen murdered in El Salvador in 1980 and the six university Jesuits with their housekeeper and her daughter killed a decade later all give a witness in the uniqueness of their own persons that is theologically identical.

Like the *imago Dei* doctrine, the *imago Christi* doctrine also works both ways. If women are genuinely baptized, if they have died and been raised "in Christ," if their suffering makes up for what is lacking in the suffering of Christ, then their capacity to represent Christ and to act "in persona Christi" is guaranteed, again without qualification. Arguments against this come from a perspective simply pervaded with patriarchal values.

To sum up: At a foundational level, women in the Church today are experiencing in the power of the Spirit that they are theomorphic and Christomorphic. It is precisely and concretely as female that they affirm their identity as *imago Dei, imago Christi*. This brings with it a strong affirmation of all the relationships with which women are personally involved: to female bodiliness and sexuality, to significant other persons, to social and economic structures, to the ecology of the earth—all enter intrinsically into women's new blessing of themselves.

WE HAVE BEEN EXPLORING an emerging new resource for promoting the greater glory of God, namely, the genuine and equal humanity of women.

In the perspective I am delineating, two options are ruled out: reverse sexism, which would place women in dominant positions to the diminishment of men; and a sameness which would level out genuine variety and particularity, disrespecting uniqueness. Rather, the goal is the flourishing of all beings in their uniqueness and interrelation—both sexes, all races and social groups, all creatures in the universe. This calls for a new model of relationship, neither a hierarchical one which requires an over/under structure, nor a univocal one which reduces all to a given norm. The model is rather inclusive, celebratory of difference, circular, feminist—we reach for the words.

What is envisioned here is a new community. Christian women hope so to change unjust structures and distorted symbol systems that a new community in church and society becomes possible, a liberating community of all women and men characterized by mutuality with each other and harmony with the earth. To reach that goal, as Rosemary Ruether has argued,

> All of us, both men and women, oppressor and oppressed, need to be converted, in somewhat different ways, to that whole humanity which has been denied to us by systems of alienation and social oppression. This fuller humanity demands not only a conversion of the self into its fuller possibilities, but a conversion of society, a transformation of those social structures that set people in opposition to each other. We seek a new social order, a new order of human-nature relations, that both mandates and incarnates mutuality.[22]

Ultimately the eschatological dream of a new heaven and new earth where justice dwells takes hold. No group dominates, and none is subordinated. All participate equally according to their gifts and being. All are mutually valued in a movement of transcending liberation, peace, and joy.

My conviction is that for this traditional eschatological dream to become reality at all, the liberation of women as genuine human persons in communities of mutuality is essential. This requires an intrinsic valuation of women as human beings, created, sinful, redeemed, with all the dignity, rights, and responsibilities which accrue as a consequence. The vision of redeemed humanity in a community of mutuality, though never fully realized, becomes more actual with every small victory, every partial move from situations of oppression to relationships of mutual respect, reciprocal valuing, and sharing in solidarity with the dispossessed. Given the present sexist situation in church and society promoted as the will of God, a spirituality of resistance and liberation accompanies the struggle.

Ad maiorem Dei gloriam; Gloria Dei vivens homo. Empowered by the Spirit, we can and must say that God's glory is realized in women's flourishing—every woman everywhere. Critically realizing the genuine humanity of the socially least of women insists upon a new configuration of theory and praxis for the benefit of all creation, human beings, and the earth. Only when the poorest, raped, and brutalized women in a black South African township, a Latin American barrio, a North American inner city—the epitome of victims of sexism, racism, and classism, and at the same time startling examples of women's resiliency, courage, love, and dignity—only when such women and their sisters around the world may live peacefully in the enjoyment of their human dignity, only then will God's glory truly be realized.

In a feminist theological perspective, women's flourishing is crucial to the greater glory of God. Without it, *homo* is incomplete, the glory of God is dishonored. If this point be granted, we are embarked on a Copernican revolution of profound proportions.

NOTES

[1] I would like to thank my colleague David Hollenbach, S.J., for materials and discussion on this point.

[2] See Anne Carr, *Transforming Grace: Women's Experience and Christian Tradition* (San Francisco: Harper and Row, 1988); Virginia Fabella & Mercy Amba Oduyoye, *With Passion and Compassion: Third World Women Doing Theology* (Maryknoll, N.Y.: Orbis, 1988); Rosemary Radford Ruether, *Sexism and God-Talk: Toward a Feminist Theology* (Boston: Beacon, 1983); Elisabeth Schüssler Fiorenza, *In Memory of Her: A Feminist Theological Reconstruction of Christian Origins* (New York: Crossroad, 1988); Elsa Tamez, ed., *Through Her Eyes: Women's Theology from Latin America* (Maryknoll, N.Y.: Orbis, 1989); and Mary Jo Weaver, *New Catholic Women* (San Francisco: Harper and Row, 1985).

[3] For biblical background, see *New Jerome Biblical Commentary*, eds. Raymond Brown, Joseph Fitzmyer, Roland Murphy (Englewood Cliffs, N.J.: Prentice Hall, 1990), pertinent texts.

[4] First draft, "Partners in the Mystery of Redemption," *Origins* 17, no. 45 (April 21, 1988): 767-88, #28; second draft, "One in Christ Jesus," *Origins* 19, no. 44 (April 5, 1990): 717-40, #34.

[5] Margaret Farley, "Sexism," *New Catholic Encyclopedia*, vol. 17, p. 604.

[6] "World's Women Data Sheet" (Washington, D.C.: Population Reference Bureau in collaboration with UNICEF, 1985).

[7] Mary Daly's *Gyn/Ecology: The Metaethics of Radical Feminism* (Boston: Beacon, 1978) explores and powerfully indicts the degradation of women in diverse cultures.

[8] The roots of Christianity's sexism in the combination of Greek philosophy and Roman law are described by Mary Collins, "The Refusal of Women in Clerical Circles," in *Women in the Church I*, Madonna Kolbenschlag, ed. (Washington, D.C.: Pastoral Press, 1987), pp. 51-63.

[9] Carol Christ, "Why Women Need the Goddess," *Womanspirit Rising*, p. 275.

[10] Robin Morgan, "Hollowmas Liturgy", in Rosemary Radford Ruether, *Women-Church: Theology and Practice* (San Francisco: Harper & Row, 1985), p. 223-28. See H.R. Trevor-Roper, *The European Witch-Craze of the Sixteenth and Seventeenth Centuries and Other Essays* (New York: Harper Torchbooks, 1969). A leading handbook for clerical inquisitors was written by Heinrich Krämer and James Sprenger, *Malleus Maleficarum*, trans. Montague Summers (New York: Dover, 1971). Background and excerpts available in Elizabeth Clark

and Herbert Richardson, eds., *Women and Religion: A Feminist Sourcebook of Christian Thought* (New York: Harper & Row, 1977), pp. 116-130. Mary Daly, *Gyn-Ecology*, pp. 178-222, traces how these deaths were viewed and subsequently ignored by Western male historians.

[11] One of the earliest and most astute analyses of this interlocking of oppressions, including race, class, and the degradation of the earth, is Rosemary Radford Ruether's *New Woman, New Earth: Sexist Ideologies and Human Liberation* (N.Y.: Seabury, 1975). See Beverly Lindsay, *Comparative Perspectives of Third World Women: The Impact of Race, Sex and Class* (New York: Praeger, 1980). The connection between suppression of women and rape of the earth is explored in Carolyn Merchant, *The Death of Nature: Women, Ecology and the Scientific Revolution* (San Francisco: Harper & Row, 1980); conversely, reverence for the earth as a component of the emancipation of women is clarified by Lois Daly, "Ecofeminism, Reverence for Life, and Feminist Theological Ethics," in *Liberating Life: Contemporary Approaches to Ecological Theology*, Charles Birch, William Eakin, Jay McDaniel, eds. (Maryknoll, N.Y.: Orbis, 1990), pp. 88-108.

[12] Gerda Lerner, *The Creation of Patriarchy* (New York: Oxford University Press, 1986).

[13] Ruether, *New Woman, New Earth*, pp. 115-33, 162-85.

[14] Bernard Lonergan, *Insight: A Study of Human Understanding* (San Francisco: Harper and Row, 1978), pp. 191-92, 222-25.

[15] *Dei Verbum* 8.

[16] Anne Carr, *Transforming Grace*, with extensive bibliography pp. 245-66.

[17] The contrast experience is described by Edward Schillebeeckx, *Christ: The Experience of Jesus as Lord*, trans. John Bowden (New York: Crossroad, 1980), passim, and used effectively throughout his *Church: The Human Story of God*, trans. John Bowden (New York: Crossroad, 1990).

[18] Karl Rahner, "Experience of Self and Experience of God," *Theological Investigations* 13, trans. David Bourke (New York: Seabury, 1975), p. 125.

[19] Ibid.

[20] Phyllis Trible, *God and the Rhetoric of Sexuality* (Philadelphia: Fortress, 1978), pp. 1-30. For negative assessment of women as *imago Dei* in the theological tradition, see Kari Elisabeth Børresen, *Subordination and Equivalence: The Nature and Role of Woman in Augustine and Thomas Aquinas* (Washington, D.C.: University Press of America, 1981).

[21] *Lumen Gentium* 42. See Sandra Schneiders, *Women and the Word: The Gender of God in the New Testament and the Spirituality of Women* (New York: Paulist, 1986).

[22] Rosemary Radford Ruether, "Feminist Theology and Spirituality," *Christian Feminism: Visions of a New Humanity*, Judith Weidman, ed. (San Francisco: Harper & Row, 1984), p. 25; and her "The Future of Feminist Theology in the Academy," *Journal of the American Academy of Religion* 53 (1985): 712.

God's Search Goes On

John W. Padberg, S.J.

MY PRESENTATION IS ABOUT QUESTIONS AND IMAGINATION. It might start with a question to me. Quite simply, what does the title of this lecture mean, "God's Search Goes On"? That title is deliberately ambiguous. Does it mean a search for God or a search by God? My reply is a question to you: "What do you think it means?" By the end of the presentation I hope you see that it means both a search for God and a search by God.

On the cover of the brochure which announced this series of lectures, there are two phrases. One is "A Spirituality for Contemporary Life," the other is "The Jesuit Heritage Today." If the Jesuit heritage today truly can be at the service of a spirituality for contemporary life, then both heritage and spirituality have to be true to their origins. Both are located in the thought and activity and prayer of Ignatius Loyola. Before I go any further, however, let me try to make clear briefly what I mean and what I do not mean by spirituality. By spirituality I do not mean "a catchall term for elevated states of feeling combined with psychological control over the nervous system and vague communing with an indeterminate and innocuous higher power—all detached from the moral choices and conduct that produce character."[1] By spirituality I do mean what we think and say and choose and do in knowing and loving and serving

God in accord with God's self-revelation in and through God's deeds, especially in the greatest of those deeds, Jesus Christ himself. By Jesuit spirituality I mean a set of particular emphases which the Society of Jesus as a whole, and individual Jesuits, and a succession of Jesuits throughout the generations have placed on some particular aspects of the doctrine and practice of Christian spirituality as a whole. In the course of these other presentations, you have heard what some of those emphases are. By Ignatian spirituality I mean something that includes those emphases but which is broader than simply Jesuit spirituality. Ignatian spirituality is the heritage of Ignatius and, I hope, of all those other men and women, Jesuits and non-Jesuits alike, who through the centuries have drawn on and enriched that heritage in their thought and works and choices and actions.

What, then, does the Ignatian spirituality of a search for God and a search by God involve for us today? More than anything else, it involves imagination and the asking of questions that go with the exercise of imagination. Imagination and questioning go hand in hand. We can hardly question a fact, a situation, a position unless we can at least begin to imagine an alternative. We can hardly imagine something new unless we ask questions about what is current. And asking questions means doing so both verbally and by the very tenor of our lives. "Saints should surprise us, . . . not confirm our moral or theological assumptions. . . . To borrow Mahatma Gandhi's justly famous phrase, the life of every genuine saint is 'an experiment with truth.'"[2] Part of that experiment with truth is to ask questions of others and of ourselves. And we shall not ourselves enrich that heritage of Ignatian spirituality without drawing on our experiences, our imaginations, and our questions.

There are all kinds of questions that might be asked in the context of Ignatian spirituality. There are too many, certainly, to take up in one presentation such as this, and one question will inevitably lead to another. But let me choose, perhaps as examples, five questions that I think are very important for current Ignatian spirituality and for its future as a resource. I shall mention them all here and then repeat them as we touch each of them in turn.

First, how do we imagine the world? That is, how do we think of the universe around us in which we look for God and God searches for us? Second, what difference to contemporary Ignatian spirituality should the psychological revolution that has taken place from Freud on for the last hundred years make in the way in which we conceive of God and self and their relationships? Third, how might the insights of the women's movement of the last several decades enrich the Jesuit heritage and help the wider Ignatian spirituality critique itself? Fourth, how do social structures influence a spirituality and how are they in turn influenced thereby? Fifth, how do we maintain and nourish for the Church a love which has both a warm heart and a clear eye?

Please do not think that I am going to give you the answers to those questions. It would be certifiable madness to think that I personally have the definitive answers. And even if I did have them, it would be crazier yet to think that I could present such answers in such a brief paper. Some of the questions several of the other presentations touched on, sometimes briefly, sometimes at greater length. But even so, I would also most falsely flatter you by suggesting that, if we all put our heads together, we would all come up with such definitive answers. We would not and we could not.

Rather, I have a more modest agenda and, I hope, a simple structure whereby to accomplish it. First, I shall ask in turn each of those five main questions and briefly elucidate and develop it by subordinate questions and simple remarks. I shall also try to give from the life of Ignatius an example of his involvement with that question. Third, I shall mention as an example from a later period of Jesuit and Ignatian spirituality a person or movement which further developed that spirituality by word or deed. I shall do so not that Ignatius or others will give us answers from the past but rather so that we may stimulate our imaginations in the face of that question today. In this way we might begin to see ourselves not so much as privileged inheritors of an Ignatian spirituality from the past but as responsible for developing that spirituality for the present and the future. Obviously, five questions will mean that I can treat each of them in only a very limited way. But I make no apologies for that because it is you who will develop them further.

We know that Ignatius referred to himself in his *Autobiography* as "the pilgrim." He started from his present circumstances and moved into the future, sometimes into new and uncharted and even dangerous territory, in his active search for God. But, however far he got on that pilgrim journey, he was utterly convinced that he could never have taken even the first step if God had not first sought him out and then accompanied him faithfully on the way, as God does with all of us too. Our responsibility, our privilege is to search for God. Our support in doing so is that God first seeks us out, starts us off, and accompanies us all the way. God's search is all gift.

LET US NOW TAKE UP THAT FIRST QUESTION. How do we imagine the world? That is, how do we think of the universe around us and the planet on which we live as we search for God and God seeks us out? As described by one of his earliest companions, Ignatius at times would sit late at night on the balcony of his room in Rome, utterly quiet, looking up at the stars and with tears coursing gently down his face. But what was this world as Ignatius knew it? It was a world with the stars moving in crystalline spheres and the sun circling an earth which was at the literal, physical center of all the created universe. That universe had come directly from God's hands, some few thousands of years before, all done in seven days. Thus did a combination of Scripture and Aristotle teach. If Ignatius had asked himself questions about the physical details of such a world, he would, I suspect, simply have accepted that cosmology as a given.

'Saints should surprise us... not confirm our moral or theological assumptions.'

Do we still have that view of our world, of our universe? Of course not, in our moments of explicit attention to science. But how about in our spiritual lives? What does it mean for our prayer that, as a matter of fact, God as creator of this universe acted not some six thousand years ago but billions and billions of years ago to produce a universe wrought perhaps by a cosmic explosion of unimaginable magnitude, the effects of which still act upon us today? What difference does it make that matter has its absolute mirror negative? Or that this planet Earth, a speck in that universe, is probably some four billion six hundred million years old. To get some sense of scale, take off the billions and keep the forty-six and count backwards. If the earth were forty-six years old, only at forty-two did the earliest plant life begin. Mammals appeared on the scene eight months ago. Modern human beings have been around for four hours of those forty-six years. During the last few hours, they discovered agriculture.

The industrial revolution began a minute ago.³ What does the Book of Genesis say to us then?

When we look more closely at the planet Earth, in those sixty seconds of biological time since the industrial revolution began, what difference to our prayers does it make that we have been responsible for the extinction of at least five hundred species of animals, ransacked the planet for fuel, and only in about the last five seconds have realized that the resources of this earth are not infinite, that we are responsible for nature in ways never imagined before, and that the Earth may go out, not with a bang but with the whimper of ever scarcer resources. What do the new developments in scientific thinking do toward recovering something like a sacramental sense of the universe that a person such as Teilhard de Chardin had? As a recent book, *The Rebirth of Nature: The Greening of Science and God*, maintains, ever since the scientific revolution we have conceived of nature as a machine, and now the newer scientific thinking connects much more with the sense of the sacred, with prayer and with ritual.⁴ In that context how do the words of Gerard Manley Hopkins resonate in our beings, "Thee God I come from, to thee go / All day long I like fountain flow / From thy hand out"? What does it mean that the Christianity we profess, now two thousand years old, is at best in its utter infancy, that we are still probably at the very beginning of the implications of God becoming a human being like us, searching us out? What does all of that mean for our prayer? As we pray the words of the Psalm, "When I look at the stars, the work of your hands," what might that mean for us, literally, and perhaps more importantly, imaginatively? How do I think of God, of Jesus, of Gospel, of Church, in the light of what the real universe around us is like? Where do the *Spiritual Exercises*, finding God in all things, the wonder of creation in the Principle and Foundation, the Contemplation to Obtain Love in which we talk about God at work in the universe, where do all of them fit? How would we translate the wonder that Ignatius felt for God's creation as he knew it to a wonder appropriate to God's creation as we know it today?

I<small>F WE WERE TO TURN NEXT FROM THE STARRY SKIES ABOVE</small> to the psychic life within, to alter slightly Immanuel Kant's phrase, we come to our second question. What difference to contemporary Ignatian spirituality should the psychological revolution that has taken place from Freud on for the last hundred years make in the way we conceive of God and self and their relationships? Again, to take an example from the life of Ignatius, recently Father William Meissner, a Jesuit and university professor of psychoanalysis at Boston College, wrote an article entitled "Becoming Ignatius." The material was drawn from a lecture series at Boston College entitled "The Psychology of a Saint." He took the events of the early life of Ignatius, up to Manresa, as examples of a powerful ego bent to a new ideal and of the remarkable resources which that ego could bring to the service of that ideal, both early in Ignatius's life and later with all the changes it underwent. He noted the narcissistic value system of the early life of Ignatius and the struggles which a new set of altruistic values imposed on him. He suggested, as to be expected, some of the psychological effects which were wrought in the pilgrim soul and some of the external indications thereof. Not only do none of these insights detract from the spiritual nature of that early struggle; rather they may help to illuminate how God was working in Ignatius.

What do the new developments in scientific thinking do toward recovering something like a sacramental sense of the universe?

Again, Ignatius makes much of discernment, as well he might. It figures greatly in his life, from his earliest conversion experience at Loyola, to the days of terror and ecstasy at Manresa, to the rules for discernment in the *Spiritual Exercises*, to his own practice of discernment as revealed in his own *Spiritual Journal.* For an example of insights from contemporary clinical psychology as an aid to discernment and as a source of critical reflection on that process, we might turn to an article in a recent issue of *Studies in the Spirituality of Jesuits* entitled "Trust Your Feelings, But Use Your Head." The article has the subtitle "Discernment and the Psychology of Decision Making." As the author remarks near the beginning of the article,

> While those employing "religious talk" speak of discerning, most of the rest of the world talks about making decisions. Interestingly enough, a wealth of information exists on both discernment and decision making. Yet each of these two bodies of literature does not

seem to know that the other exists. Or at least they are not acknowledging and communicating with one another.[5]

Yet, precisely as men and women concerned with decision making both in our spiritual lives and in our ordinary workaday world, if we wish to make that distinction, it would help us to know at least something about the relation of affect and intellect, or about a psychological model for sound decision making, or about the reciprocal influences of cognition and emotion, or about the role of expectations, or about attribution theory, or about heuristics, "rules of thumb," in the face of uncertainty.

I am not suggesting that we have to be clinical psychologists in order to deal with discernment. But when we speak of discernment and the rules of discernment as among the great gifts of Ignatius to Christian spirituality, we would falsify the gifts if we neglect the knowledge which has been accumulated over the last century from a discipline such as psychology, unknown in Ignatius's day. As we search for God and God's actions and as God seeks the response of our lives, the more we integrate into that search the ongoing growth of knowledge of the human psyche, the better.

M<small>OVE NOW TO THE THIRD QUESTION</small>. How might the insights of the women's movement of the last several decades enrich the Jesuit heritage and help the wider Ignatian spirituality to critique itself? Hugo Rahner's great compilation of letters and commentaries, entitled *Saint Ignatius Loyola: Letters to Women*, has much enriched our understanding of Ignatius and of his times and of the people, both women and men, who were his contemporaries. The book was originally published in Germany in 1956 at the four hundredth anniversary of the death of St. Ignatius. Some time after publication, the then general of the Society of Jesus asked Father Rahner why, of all the things that he might have done to commemorate that four hundredth anniversary, he had chosen this topic of Ignatius's letters to women. Father Rahner replied (and we must note that the question came shortly after the first Sputnik had gone up into space), "Father General, it is just like the other side of the moon. Until recently, we never had the opportunity to see it."

But the very first experience of pastoral work which Ignatius had was with women. To middle-class Spanish housewives and ladies of the country nobility, Ignatius at Manresa spoke the things of God.

At Barcelona, as early as 1523, Ignatius met Isabel Roser, one of his very greatest benefactors and a woman of whom he said, in a letter in 1532, that "there was not a woman in the world to whom I owe more." From 1524 to 1526 he learned at Barcelona to give spiritual direction to women who, even twenty to thirty years later, would remember him with affection. At Alcalá in 1527, when he was a student, he had, among the women with whom he worked, widows and wives of artisans and maidservants and apprentice girls and even one who said, "I was one of the lost. I was very wicked, keeping company with students." After 1537 Ignatius's life was centered on Rome, but even in the midst of all of the work there of founding the Society of Jesus and writing its Constitutions, he again took up the spiritual direction of men and women and he became increasingly famous for it. In addition, he was probably the first Jesuit marriage counselor, called upon frequently to restore peace between husband and wife, Margaret of Austria, the daughter of Charles V, and Ottavio Farnese, the grandson of Pope Paul III. Some of that spiritual direction he carried on by correspondence. But there were all kinds of other letters too. In about five hundred printed pages of his correspondence with women, royal ladies, noble ladies, benefactresses, spiritual directees, mothers of fellow Jesuits, and women who were his friends, Ignatius, to quote Hugo Rahner, "becomes alive, with that humanity without which there is no holiness in the Church of a God made one of us."[6]

In the *Spiritual Exercises*, at that very important first contemplation of the Second Week, the one on the Incarnation, the whole world of humanity, the Trinity, and Mary herself are at its center. The very first contemplation of the Fourth Week is entitled, simply and directly, "How Christ Our Lord Appeared to Our Lady," and then Ignatius goes on to remark, seemingly with a slight edge to his voice, "This, although it is not said in Scripture, is included in saying that He appeared to so many others, because Scripture supposes that we have understanding. . . ."[7]

All well and good, but it is unfortunate that Ignatius was unable sufficiently to break loose from his own times and imagine what an independent, apostolic career for women might mean, both for women religious and lay women. Of course, even if he could have done so, there is no evidence that the social circumstances in which women found themselves at the time would have allowed such a career.

Neither the experience of the brief career as a Jesuit of that great woman benefactor, Isabel Roser, nor the experience of the longer but completely secret career as a Jesuit of Juana, princess of Spain, could contribute to his breaking free of unexamined preconceptions. Why that was so, and the story of these two women who were Jesuits, would be the subject of a complete lecture in itself. Given his own experience and the circumstances of the time, it became impossible for Ignatius, a man otherwise so capable of seeing innovative ideas and fitting them into the context of a sound tradition, to ask whether the forms of the religious life, not only for men but also for women, had to be changed to fit the context of a sixteenth-century world radically different from the world in which the vocation of women religious had begun, taken root, and flourished. Certainly some women saw what it could mean to be an active religious woman in the service of the Church. Angela Merici and Mary Ward, "that incomparable woman," as Pius XII called her, saw what it could mean to be an apostolic order of women. The six almost anonymous women who helped to found the Congregation of St. Joseph in the seventeenth century and the extraordinary women who founded such a great variety of apostolic congregations in the nineteenth century enlarged the whole idea of what women might do on their own in the service of the Lord.

To be obviously anachronistic for a moment, it is too bad that Ignatius did not have the immense good fortune to have an Angela Merici or a Mary Ward or a Jeanne de Chantal or a Louise de Marillac or a Madeleine Sophie Barat or a Caroline Gerhardinger to help him see what a women's apostolic religious order might be. It is too bad that a laywoman in the world such as Dorothy Day was not available to Ignatius as a model for the several groups of laywomen who tried to become involved in apostolic activities outside cloister or home. The history of the life of women religious and of laywomen in the Church might have been different. But here we are in the twentieth century. What has the experience of at least the last century of directly apostolic orders of women and of simply individual lay women in so great a variety of works taught us? What has their imagination taught all of us? How have their questions stimulated our imaginations in turn? How has "Christian tradition and women's experience" been for us, to use the title of Anne Carr's excellent book, a "transforming grace"?[8]

But, ranging beyond simply the activities of the Church, what has the more generalized women's movement of the last decades taught us about the varieties of ways in which the human person searches for God, or about how God acts on men and women, or about how sexism is as much a block as other "isms" to our understanding of each other, and to our work with each other, and to the further development of an Ignatian spirituality that should value equally the experiences of both women and men? (These questions, written several weeks before this lecture series began, were at least in part responded to in the lecture by Elizabeth Johnson.)

To be quite frank, those questions are often not easy to deal with in many instances in Ignatian spirituality. To take one simple example: How does one deal imaginatively with the overwhelmingly masculine language of the *Spiritual Exercises*? There is at least one translation that attempts to remove any and all sex-specific language. Right now the Institute of Jesuit Sources is working on a new translation of the *Exercises* and finding out how hard it is to maintain the integrity of a classic text and at the same time to shed the gender particularities expressive of the age when that text was written. I invite you to try it. We hope we shall eventually succeed.

> *It is unfortunate that Ignatius was unable sufficiently to break loose from his own times and imagine what an independent, apostolic career for women might mean.*

But, much more than in the text of the *Spiritual Exercises*, it is in the script of our lives as men and women in the Church that we will help bring about the equality of women and men that the Church proclaims but does not yet live. How will the heritage of Ignatian spirituality help to bring that about? Bernard Lonergan speaks of "the work of the free and responsible agent producing the first and only edition of oneself."[9] What does your imagination see as to the ways in which many such selves will write that script?

LET US TURN NOW TO THE FOURTH QUESTION. How do social structures influence Ignatian spirituality and how are they in turn influenced thereby? It may have become a truism that social, economic, and political structures impinge upon a spirituality, but let us become more specific than that by taking an example. How does American individualism, and the structures that over the decades we have set in place to foster that individualism, influence our reading of the Ignatian text and the living out of the Ignatian heritage, both positively and negatively? What makes an American reading of the *Spiritual Exercises* different from an Indonesian or Polish or Zambian or Salvadoran reading? What habits of the heart, to allude to the title of that important work by Robert Bellah, do we bring to our search for God? What such habits does God have to take into account in searching us out? What in our socioeconomic and political structures blinds us to the fundamental choices we make, the standards we choose, or the paths on which we are journeying? What in those structures supports and helps us in those choices on that journey?

> *It is in the script of our lives as men and women in the Church that we will help bring about the equality of women and men that the Church proclaims but does not yet live.*

A study of the Ignatian heritage with fresh eyes can yield unexpected results here too. As the recent study "Saint, Site and Sacred Strategy" says,

> Both modern critical theory and common sense teach that in order to understand the past, the events and the people involved in them must be read and interpreted within their social, political, religious and economic context. Only by entering into this hermeneutical circle—a return to the sources and contexts—can meaning be appropriated from the past in order to address the pressing issues of the present.[10]

The particular study that I just quoted from is part of the catalog of an exhibit in the Vatican Library at the present time entitled, "Ignatius, Rome and Jesuit Urbanism." With a fresh eye to the evidence, the author argues that the urban vision of Ignatius in Rome of the 1540s and 1550s influenced his choice of place and ministries and apostolates and helped shape the Ignatian spirituality that was in process of development. The author starts with the old Jesuit headquarters and the great church of the Gesù in the center of Rome and demonstrates how Ignatius situated those institutions at that point in Rome where devotion to the Church, desire to influence society, and work with the least fortunate intersected—or, as he puts it in another way, in close proximity to popes, politicians, and prostitutes.

That whole study is a good example of looking at Ignatian spirituality with fresh eyes. It has long been known that Ignatius wrote more than seven thousand letters in the course of his life, more than Luther and Calvin combined. Some of them contained the deepest teachings on prayer and religious life, but about a thousand of them also are on real estate. In some ways they mirror Ignatius himself, who could recount a striking, mystical awareness of God that suddenly came upon him on a Roman street corner right after seeing a prominent citizen on business.

As an example of politics touching our prayer, I am sure we all prayed recently that peace might come to the Middle East. Without discounting the genuineness of those prayers, still that was an easy thing to do, to pray for peace there. When, however, is the last time we looked at a serious sociological study of our urban metropolitan area or got concerned about the coming school-board elections? Both such a study and such elections have something to say about how and where the Gospel can be preached and even whether it can be preached fruitfully in our own social environment here and now. We may well have made the ultimate choice to which the meditation in the *Spiritual Exercises* on the Two Standards invites us, but how can we make the proximate choices that carry forward the standard we have chosen, if we do not even know the circumstances that influence our choices and the circumstances in which we can or cannot carry them out?

FINALLY, OUR LAST QUESTION: How do we maintain and nourish for the Church a love which has both a warm heart and a clear eye? To put it quite directly, in the very words of Ignatius that stand near the beginning of the Formula of the Institute, the fundamental "Rule" of the Society of Jesus, the role of the Society is "to serve the Lord alone and the Church, His spouse, under the Roman Pontiff, the vicar of Christ on earth."[11] And near the end of the *Spiritual Exercises*, he has a set of Rules for Thinking with the Church, or probably better expressed, Rules for Thinking in the Church. Yes, those rules are bound at least in part to the times and circumstances and expressions of the sixteenth century. Yes, those very phrases of the Formula of the Institute come in part out of an ecclesiology that has surely undergone development. For example, Vatican II calls not only the pope but also the bishops "vicars of Christ," and that surely needs careful exegesis. But there is no gainsaying the fact that Ignatius did reverence and seek to serve the pope, and did love the Church. And that is all the more remarkable in that he was well aware of the less-than-admirable personal character of many of the popes of his lifetime, and had had run-ins with the cardinal who was to be Pope Paul IV, and had been subjected to eight legal processes from the Inquisition and other Church offices from 1526 up to just before the Society of Jesus was founded. No wonder that early in the *Spiritual Exercises* Ignatius says, "It is necessary to suppose that every good Christian is more ready to put a good interpretation on another's statement than to condemn it as false."[12]

As for the very direct way Ignatius asks us to think with the Church and the Holy See, a single set of examples on two values central for Ignatius and briefly summed up here will give us material for reflection on how Ignatius thought that attitude ought to be carried out in practice. Value one: reverence and obedience to the pope and putting on the mind of the Church. Value two: the absolute refusal of any ecclesiastical dignities, such as becoming bishops or cardinals, by members of the nascent Society of Jesus.[13] At least eight times in Ignatius's lifetime such offers were made by the Holy See to early Jesuits, and it was clear in at least several of them that the pope was directly and explicitly involved in the offers. In every case Ignatius opposed the offers and did everything he could to make them inoperative. For example, in the instance of making Jay, one of the first Jesuits, a bishop, Ignatius wrote memoranda, visited influential cardinals, lobbied Paul III's secretary, visited the pope himself, asked civil officials to intervene, and even got Margaret of Austria, the wife of the pope's grandson, to write a note to His Holiness, and prayed and got others to pray against the move. He succeeded in stopping it.

Another example: When several times Pope Julius III wanted to make Francis Borgia a cardinal, Ignatius went through the same routine and even got Princess Juana, the secret Jesuit scholastic, to persuade her brother, Philip II, to intervene. Ignatius said after prayer that the matter was so clear to him that "even if the whole world were to fall prostrate at his feet, he would try his utmost to prevent the promotion."[14]

The same was true of Laínez, also one of the first Jesuits, at several attempts to make him a bishop or a cardinal. Of one of those attempts, Pedro Ribadeneira, an early Jesuit, says that Ignatius told him, "If our Lord does not interfere, we shall have Master Laínez as a cardinal. But I guarantee you that, if this does happen, it will occur with such a protest that the whole world will understand whether the Society seeks red hats and miters or strives to avoid them."[15]

What are we to make of all this? Much more than I can possibly deal with here. It simply suggests that examples such as these might be very important for our understanding of reverence for the pope, obedience to his wishes, service of the Holy See, and "thinking with the Church." But we would totally falsify such an understanding if we took it out of the context of the unquestioned love of the Church that Ignatius had. It was not an idealized church existing in some ethereal never-never land, but this Church of his own age, a Church which had an unusual number of faults. I would suggest that the phrase "realistic reverence" would sum up his attitude in this complicated question, and that another phrase, this time from St. Paul, would sum up how he sought to act, "doing the truth in love."[16] Finding the truth is not always easy. Doing the truth is harder yet because we are all too inclined to find our own truth all too easily. Doing the truth in love is the most difficult of all. But I honestly think that such is the only way we shall help make the Church what it ought to be.

Ignatius situated his institutions in close proximity to popes, politicians, and prostitutes.

Two examples from more recent times are for me personally among the most striking. In the early 1950s, a group of Jesuits and Dominicans in France were under suspicion from the Vatican as proponents of "la nouvelle théologie," the so-called new theology. Several of them such as Yves Congar and Jean Daniélou and Henri de Lubac were at least indirectly censured and effectively silenced. In several instances Church officials removed them or forced them from their teaching posts. In that very context, de Lubac could still sit down and write one of the most remarkable scholarly—and at the same time personal—statements of what the Church was and why it was eminently an object of love and devotion, in his book translated as *The Splendor of the Church*. An even more recent example of doing the truth in love was Pedro Arrupe, the father general of the Society of Jesus who died February 5, 1991. In the experience of contemporary Jesuits, here was a person who faced the truth as it became evident, who passionately loved the Church, and who honestly spoke and did the truth in that love.

EACH OF THE FIVE QUESTIONS ASKED HERE could easily be the subject of its own lecture. Indeed, each has been the subject of book-length treatments and, just as importantly, the subject of lived experience. I have posed those questions this evening not, as I said earlier, to provide answers but to stimulate imaginations on how the Jesuit heritage might be a resource for contemporary spirituality in this world of ours. I am convinced that it can truly be so only if that heritage enters into living contact with that contemporary world. The five questions of this presentation do not exhaust the opportunities and the problems of our world, nor are they necessarily always the most important questions. But they do at least bring to the forefront of our consciousness the physical world around us, the psychological world within us, the world of at least half the human race, the world in which we set up the structures of our social interaction, and the world of the Church, the community of believers whose life, by God's good grace, we share.

> *It was not an idealized church existing in some ethereal never-never land, but this Church of his own age, a Church which had an unusual number of faults.*

You will have noticed, too, that these five questions summon up to memory five important pieces of the *Spiritual Exercises*, and no one need remark that the *Exercises* are the central heritage of the Society of Jesus. The first or cosmological question of creation relates to the Principle and Foundation and to the Contemplation to Attain God's Love. The second or psychological question relates to the "discernment of spirits." The question about women in the Church relates to the centrality of a particular woman, Mary, in the meditations on the Incarnation and the Resurrection and to the equally central place women as much as men ought to hold in the ongoing life of the Church. The societal question suggests that in the concrete the Two Standards must present themselves to us in the context of social structures. And finally, the last question on the Church obviously connects with those celebrated Rules for Thinking with the Church. How imaginatively can that Jesuit heritage then provide us with resources for a contemporary spirituality? The answer depends on us. To make it such a resource, we shall have to "unite respect for tradition and the imagination to enlarge it, the prudence to be faithful and the courage to be critical."[17]

That heritage began with Ignatius Loyola. To him, then, I return as I near the conclusion of this talk. In between the beginning of that heritage and today, Ignatius's gifts to the Church have been developed and enriched over the centuries by women and men who have fashioned what we call Ignatian spirituality. We say that that spirituality seeks to find God in all things. And through all things God searches for us and our response to his love. But we can seek and respond fully only if we today share in a characteristic that Pope Gregory XV called attention to when Ignatius was canonized in 1622. He said that Ignatius was a saint not because of his administrative abilities or his psychological insights or his courage, but finally because, as he grew in response to God's loving search for him, "he had a heart big enough to contain the whole wide world."

As I began with a question, so let me end. What better could we imagine asking of God or what more could God want to give us as central to the heritage we hand on to contemporary Ignatian spirituality than such "a heart big enough to contain the whole wide world"?

NOTES

[1] Kenneth L. Woodward, *Making Saints* (New York: Simon and Schuster, 1990), p. 396.

[2] Mohandas Gandhi, *An Autobiography: Or the Story of My Experiments with Truth* (Boston: Beacon Press, 1968), in Woodward, ibid.

[3] See *The Tablet*, May 19, 1990, p. 625, for these and further details.

[4] Rupert Sheldrake, *The Rebirth of Nature: The Greening of Science and God* (New York: Bantam Books, 1990).

⁵ Michael J. O'Sullivan, S.J., "Trust Your Feelings but Use Your Head: Discernment and the Psychology of Decision Making," *Studies in the Spirituality of Jesuits* 22/4, September 1990.

⁶ Hugo Rahner, S.J., *Saint Ignatius Loyola: Letters to Women* (New York: Herder and Herder, 1960), p. 1.

⁷ *Spiritual Exercises*, [218] and [299].

⁸ Anne E. Carr, B.V.M., *Transforming Grace: Christian Tradition and Women's Experience* (New York: Harper and Row, 1989).

⁹ Bernard Lonergan, S.J., *A Second Collection* (Philadelphia: Westminster Press, 1975), p. 83, as quoted in Frederick E. Crowe, S.J., "Son of God, Holy Spirit and World Religions," Chancellor's Address, Toronto, Regis College, 1984, p. 39.

¹⁰ Thomas M. Lucas, S.J., "Ignatius, Rome, and the Jesuit Urban Mission," in *Saint, Site and Sacred Strategy* (Rome: Biblioteca Apostolica Vaticana, 1990), p. 17.

¹¹ Formula of the Institute [3].

¹² *Spiritual Exercises* [22].

¹³ See *Constitutions* [756] and [817-818].

¹⁴ See MHSI, *EpMixtae*, III, 403-406.

¹⁵ Pedro Ribadeneira, S.J., *Vida del P. Maestro Diego Laínez* (Madrid: BAC, 1945), vol. 1, p. 10.

¹⁶ Ephesians 4:15

¹⁷ Leo J. O'Donovan, S.J., "An Invitation to Explore," in *Georgetown* (winter 1990), p. 24.